THE
GIVING ZONE

ENTER THE REALM WHERE YOUR DREAMS COME TRUE

Bruce Painter

BY BRUCE PAINTER

In The Zone Press
1400 Camp Letoli Road
Saint Jo, Texas 76265
1-866-319-7736
ba.painter@comcast.net

ISBN: 1-4243-0026-6

Book Design by Jonathan Gullery,
RJ Communications
jg@budgetbookdesign.com

Printed in the United States of America

*This book is dedicated to Shoshana –
my wife, partner and best friend.
You have been a great teacher who has shown me
the way to give unconditionally,
and love with a boundless heart.*

ACKNOWLEDGEMENTS

It took a lot of people to make this book happen. This book comes from my deep study, and my learning from many people who have had an impact on my life. I stand on the shoulders of many who have paved the way before me.

I have special gratitude for the key mentor in my life, Alan C. Walter, who has spent countless hours at a profound level researching the human spirit, and who has conveyed to me the level of awareness that has made this book possible.

I thank Eric Wolery for the years of very valuable mentoring and friendship that helped prepare me for a successful life.

I thank my colleagues and friends from the Advanced Coaching and Leadership Center – Maureen Mahoney, Ceil Stanford, Joel Haggar, Jolee Ferreira, Barbara Kalb and Lola Wolery – for the vital positive influence they have had on my life. I want to thank all the students around the world connected to the Advanced Coaching and Leadership Center who have helped me progress in my life's dreams and aspirations.

I also extend my appreciation to Loy and Robert Young for their mentoring and the very special gift of helping my wife and me get together to form a very strong relationship.

A warm thank-you to my development editor, Janis Hunt Johnson, who not only has done a superb job of editing, and mentoring, but has also contributed to the book immensely through her writing skills and great wisdom.

Thanks to my brother, Terry Painter, who has been an inspiration in my life when it comes to business ingenuity, humor, and love.

My deepest thanks go to my mother, Genevieve Painter, who had a profound influence on me to get into the field of helping people and was a great model of service to humanity.

CONTENTS

INTRODUCTION

What quality does a person need to develop in order to have the most successful and happy life possible?

I believe the answer to that question is the ability to freely give to others.

I realize that there are many other great qualities one could choose to answer this question.

I have been on a personal development quest since 1968 as a student and since 1972 as a speaker, consultant and trainer.

The quality that I observe in the world as being utmost in importance to all other qualities is the ability to give freely. This is not only what I've observed in many other people, but also what I have observed profoundly in my own life.

To *give* means "to make a present of, bestow, grant, contribute, impart, donate, or deliver in exchange or in recompense." The process of giving is involved in virtually every human interaction. Without the process of giving, and its counterpart, the process of receiving, nearly everything would be at a standstill.

The greatest changes in my life that have affected my success and happiness have had to do with greatly increasing the amount

I have given of myself to others. This giving on my part has also most often had a dramatic positive effect on the people to whom I have given.

When I seriously increase how much I give of myself, my world changes to a much better world. I enter into what I call "The Giving Zone" where life becomes joyful, loving, fun, successful, prosperous, and purposeful.

I have used the word "Zone" in the title because many of us have had winning experiences of "being in the zone." This is the experience athletes hit when everything goes right in their game – a football player, for example, completes nine passes in a row.

"Being in the zone" can also describe the experience of a salesperson who, for example, makes 20 sales in a row and sets a company record. It can also describe the joy of a husband and wife who work to improve their relationship and fall as deeply in love as they were prior to their marriage.

The word "zone" has been used frequently in the publications and recordings of Alan C. Walter. In his book, *The Secrets to Increasing Your Power, Wealth and Happiness*, Walter uses the term "the Green Zone" to describe:

...someone who is in the right place at the right time, making things go right. This person is living his dream... very successful, happy and prosperous.

Watch Oprah Winfrey at work as she fully pours her heart out to help transform the lives of the many people she touches. Her supreme ability and desire to give has been a large part of her success and has made her one of the most loved people in America. She lives "in the zone" and is clearly also in The Giving Zone.

Mother Teresa was exemplary in her life of giving. She founded and nourished a vast organization of helpers and raised huge sums of money to help multitudes of people. She was certainly a permanent resident in The Giving Zone.

Whether it is the superstar athlete who finds self-fulfillment through dedication to a charitable organization, or the business executive who is on a mission to market a product that improves the quality of our lives, the ability to give fully and freely is paramount to maximizing the quality and effectiveness of our lives.

Giving encompasses many areas of our lives, including giving to our family, our friends, our career, our hobbies, our religious organizations, our favorite charities, our pets, and our environment.

An important motivation behind the writing of this book was the major shift I made in my life to give more to others. The shift was phenomenal. My life was revolutionized from mediocrity, dreariness, and some selfishness to a heightened sense of accomplishment, happiness, and service. The quality of my marriage, friendships, and career improved. Life became a much more meaningful and exciting adventure. I began to experience more of being "in the zone" – The Giving Zone – an extraordinary realm of existence.

Another impetus behind the writing of this book came from my observation of influential people who make a very positive difference in the lives of many. I feel that if there is one quality that separates them from the rest, it is their unstoppable spirit of giving.

I believe that when we greatly increase the amount we give, other important character traits will also improve dramatically. A few of these traits may include self-discipline, perseverance, enthusiasm, a hunger for knowledge, and love. For example, when we shift from focusing on ourselves to a passionate focus on a worthy cause, our individual self-discipline will be boosted because of that passionate focus. Another example is, when people shift their focus toward more giving to others, they automatically increase their connectedness to others. Their love and compassion for others also increases.

Because of my own experience and through observing the lives of others, I have come to the following conclusion:

*When people give passionately and unboundedly in the direction
of a chosen purpose, the realization of that purpose will come into
fruition at a greatly accelerated rate.*

The problem is that many people suppress their ability to give. They have a fear about giving or a reluctance to give.

What is behind this fear or reluctance to give? We will explore this question and more. The main focus of the book is to share my understanding of the giving process and how it works, and to show you how to increase your capacity to give, plus have the deep and rewarding experience of living in The Giving Zone.

Each chapter contains a subject that can highly contribute to your ability to give. There are many other benefits to be gleaned from each chapter of the book. These include some people skills, communication skills, and business skills that relate to the process of giving.

We will look at some of the causes behind a reluctance to give as well as some forces that empower giving. What can you do if you give freely to someone close to you, and that person does not give anything back? What do you do if the people you give to become dependent on you, and do nothing to stand on their own two feet? How do you inspire other people to want to give? How important is it for you to become proficient in your ability to receive? How do you greatly improve your ability to give, even if you are already skilled at giving?

As you read through the book, you are encouraged to inspect the material and draw your own conclusions. Of course, it is written from my perspective and some of that perspective may not be true for you. It is healthy to disagree. Discernment is invaluable and essential when reading.

The people who will get the most benefit from this book, and enjoy it to its fullest, are those who have an open mind to new ideas. Since you've picked up this book, it sets you apart as one who actively seeks knowledge and wants to improve.

We'll have very little improvement in our lives if we only stick to what we know. Some of the ideas in this book may be new and different to you. They are intended to be highly interesting, novel, enlightening, and immediately practical in everyday life.

It is very helpful to look up any words that aren't familiar to you in a good dictionary. The understanding of such words will greatly magnify the value you get out of this book.

Please also feel free to read this book many times. I have found that when I read a book more than once, each time I increase my understanding significantly. It's amusing that sometimes I'll read a book again and some of it I will not recognize as having read it before. This is because I have a much deeper understanding of the subject and can now see sections that seem new to me because I simply didn't comprehend them before.

Also this is not one of those self-help books that promises quick fixes and instant changes in your life. It's more about the steady, lasting type of changes that come from gaining knowledge, developing skills, developing character, and practicing and gaining mastery. It is also about the fun, fulfillment, and happiness that come from increasing your commitment to giving to others.

When reading *The Giving Zone* pay particular attention to Chapter 1. It is about an invaluable concept that transformed my life and the lives of many others, and it is pivotal to the value you will receive from reading the rest of the book.

In the book I share personal examples. They are not written to boast about myself, but as valuable teaching tools. You will find out that I've been far from perfect. Like everyone else, I've erred often in my life and have had opportunities to learn from my mistakes.

One of my biggest lessons in life came when I gave up a reluctance to give and discovered the experience, fun, and joy of giving. The perspective of having experienced both sides has been invaluable in the writing of this book.

I do not make any claims of being a great expert or a master in the area of giving. My expertise is a result of having experienced both sides of this perspective – non-giving as well as giving. In addition, I share many valuable processes that I have observed, experienced, studied, and taught that increase our ability to give, and thus greatly increase the quality of our lives and make a better world.

The Giving Zone is designed for those who are already very strong in giving freely as well as for those who have some reluctance about giving.

I wish that those who have been through a lot of personal growth or who already have a large capacity to give will find at least a few chapters that will help unlock an even greater ability to give.

For those who are new to personal growth or who have some reluctance to give, the author intends that you will discover for yourselves a greater understanding of the giving process and be able to choose ways to increase your ability to give.

I attribute the vast majority of the material in this book to my study and training for the past 16 years with a major mentor of mine – Alan C. Walter, an international renowned researcher, trainer, coach, and writer, and a very good friend. In 1989 he invited me to learn some very special knowledge and skills, many of which I share in this book. He is a great model of how best to express the spirit of giving – and he is the most dedicated person I've ever met in his work, which is to help others reach their highest potential.

In the following pages you can look forward to reading about new, powerful, and practical areas of discovery. You will join forerunners possessing advanced knowledge that will help you and those connected to you to make a better world.

For those of you who would enjoy going to even greater depth in the understanding and application of the material in this book, I've included exercises at the end of each chapter. These exercises are designed to do by yourself, or you can also do them with another person. If you have another person working with you, have that person read the statements and questions. Share each answer verbally with your partner. There is great value in that. When you share your answers with another it magnifies the results because of the other person's involvement. Then switch roles, where you read the statements and questions for your partner to answer.

I recommend that you do not change the wording of the statements or questions. They are designed to be answered just as they are. If you are working with a partner and ask the questions, – just listen and do not judge or evaluate the other person's answers.

If you have questions on any of the exercises, or questions about anything else in the book, my contact information is in the back of the book. I will be glad to help answer your questions.

The Giving Zone is designed with the aim of adding great value to the lives of those who read it. The pathway to giving will take you on an exciting adventure. Giving is a natural process. And the Giving Zone is a natural place to be. Yet, there are many individuals who, deep inside, have placed shackles on their ability to give. As each individual is freed from the prison that binds a natural human propensity to give, many others are set free.

Enjoy the adventure of *The Giving Zone*.

CHAPTER 1

BEING IN THE ZONE

"An original life is unexplored territory. You don't get there by taking a taxi – you get there by carrying a canoe."
—Alan Alda

This is a chapter of pivotal importance. I urge you to read it several times. It contains the most important concept I've learned in my life. The insights that you will gain are likely to be invaluable to you, your family, associates, and friends. It will help you increase your ability to create a fun, contributing, successful, prosperous, and happy life.

I will share more here on the definition of the word *give*, since this is a book about giving. Again, give means "to make a present of, bestow, grant, contribute, impart, donate, or deliver in exchange or in recompense." Additional meanings are "to devote or apply completely," and "to entrust to another."

Thus, giving to others can range from giving a present, to complimenting someone, to helping a friend solve a problem, or giving to a charity, or giving a service in exchange for money, or even fully listening to someone or giving your love to someone.

The key to giving, and actually the key to anything we want to do, is largely the ability to direct where we want to go in life. The ability to direct our lives is for the most part responsible for our success.

If we are in a jet plane, we want the pilot to be able to direct the plane to get us safely to our destination.

A patient receiving a heart transplant wants the heart surgeon to successfully direct the medical staff to complete a successful operation.

If we want our business to be successful, we need to direct our marketing efforts to drive customers to purchase our product.

If we want a successful marriage, we need to be able to direct our focus and abilities to give our spouse what is needed and promised, and to follow policies that make for a successful marriage.

If we want to have a fun night out with our family, we need to be able to direct our attention on selecting a fun activity and gathering the family for this purpose.

The president of a large charitable organization must have the ability to direct the efforts of hundreds of thousands of people nationally to raise the much-needed funds.

An Academy award–winning film director must have the skill to be able to direct the hundreds of people on the movie set to make an award-winning film.

We are all directors of our own movie — our lives.

As Shakespeare has said:

All the world's a stage,
And all the men and women merely players.
They have their exits and their entrances,
And one man in his time plays many parts,
His acts being seven ages.

There is a problem, however. Most people have stage productions that do not succeed, and they fall short as directors of failed marriages, depressing careers, financial debt, etc.

The vast majority of people are not directing the Academy award—winning stage productions they truly desire.

There is the couple who falls deeply in love and have fairy-tale dreams. They decide to co-direct a stage production of a loving family, prosperity, and lasting happiness. Instead their production shifts dramatically in act two — an unfaithful spouse, separation, and heartbreak.

An inspired group of friends come together and decide to co-direct a stage production of starting their own successful art business. Act one begins with the creation of a flourishing business dream. However, act two drastically transforms into a scene of betrayal of trust, bankruptcy, and liquidation.

Why do so many people have failed dreams or lead desperate lives of struggle?

The answer is that they have not gained the knowledge that would give them the ability to direct their lives successfully.
The most important question in this book is:

How do we learn to direct our lives successfully and consistently? Or how do we learn to direct our lives to create the masterpieces of the Academy award–winning stage productions we truly desire?

For most of my life, I did not really know how to direct my life. I was inconsistent in the results in my life. Sometimes I'd win and sometimes I'd lose. I experienced confusion, chaos, and disappointment. So many things seemed to happen randomly. I didn't know what the answer was.

I was fortunate to be introduced to Alan C. Walter, who shared the answer that helped me have a way to put order in my life. He said:

The answer lies in our ability to learn to run the right processes.

The definition of *process* is: "1. A system of operations in the production of something. 2. A series of actions, changes or functions that bring about an end or result. 3. Course or passage of time. 4. Ongoing movement: progression."

For our purposes let's use definition 2: "A series of actions, changes or functions that bring about an end or result."

Walter further clarifies the term *process*:

Inside any game many activities and events are occurring simultaneously. They may appear to be random and uncontrolled, but in actuality they are all being caused by someone. To fully understand what is taking place, you need to understand that each participant is engaged in a series of processes.

Everything we do has a result. Therefore everything we do is a process, whether we are aware of it or not.

The question is whether it is a process that is beneficial or detrimental. There are two types of processes. A *positive process* is a series of actions or changes or functions that brings about your intended end or result. A *negative process* is a series of actions or changes or functions that counter or prevent you from reaching your intended end or result.

Examples:

Positive Process – *You order a catered event for some guests who are coming to your home. The food turns out great, just as you wanted.*

Negative Process – *You order a catered event for some guests who are coming to your home. The caterers show up two hours late and half your guests have left before the food is served.*

Positive Process – *A new employee is learning a new production method in the company and he still isn't quite doing it right. His boss encourages him and helps him so he masters it in a short time.*

Negative Process – *The new employee learning a new production method is scolded by his boss for not doing it perfectly right away. He is discouraged and very unhappy about his new job.*

Again, every action, everything that happens, involves a process. Even something done unconsciously involves a process.

The *unconscious* processes are the processes that we need to become aware of. They run our lives – and many of them are destructive.

For example, people who are continually broke will unconsciously be driven to select or run processes to be broke – spend more than earned, accumulate credit card debt, be behind in bills, etc.

Those who have a bad temper will unconsciously select or run processes to make sure that they get upset with others – argue, tell others that they are wrong, blame, etc.

People who fear rejection will unconsciously run processes to be rejected by others – being cold, showing disinterest in others, only thinking about themselves, etc.

Walter adds:

For something to happen, someone has to make it happen.

No matter what happens, people are consciously or unconsciously making things happen. Thus, we are always running processes to make things happen whether we are aware of it or not. Another way of looking at it is that we are always directing our stage production, knowingly, or unknowingly. Again, most people actually are not in charge of directing their own lives. Other people are really directing their lives and their stage productions.

Continuing the example about people who are broke: They are not running their own lives – the banks, bill collectors, credit card services, etc., are running their lives.

You are either in charge of your life or others are in charge of your life. You are either consciously choosing processes to direct your life toward positive outcomes or others are choosing processes for you – and they may not be directing you where you truly want to go.

The magical key is to become aware of the processes we are running, and then select the best processes to get the most favorable outcomes we desire. We can become masterful directors who create great productions, and even Academy award–winning performances.

Eighteen years ago I was introduced to the concept of process. The understanding of this concept has produced monumental changes in my life and the people with whom I come in contact. As I shared earlier, my life used to be much more chaotic, and it seemed random. I have much more certainty and stability because I now understand that everything that happens is a result of a process in motion.

I have the tools to solve problems that I didn't have before. When I have a problem in a relationship, for example, I spot the process I'm running – probably a negative process such as blame – and I choose a positive process such as sharing how I am contributing to the problem. I can also spot the negative processes other people are running and help them choose positive processes. Thus I have much more harmony now in my life.

Learning to choose correct positive processes has also helped me to be more successful. In addition, I've also become more giving – a person who naturally loves to give. Even though I still have plenty of challenges and problems to solve, I'm so much more able to solve them.

Selecting and running the right processes is the key to being "in the zone." Selecting and running correct processes having to do with contributing to others is the key to being in The Giving Zone.

The chapters in this book each contain powerful positive processes that contribute to our ability to give and at the same time to create successful, prosperous, and happy lives.

We can learn to direct our lives to get the results we want for ourselves as well as for our families, careers, society, the nation, and the world. Choosing and running the correct processes is the special key to being a player on the stage of The Giving Zone.

CHAPTER 1 EXERCISE

The purpose of this exercise is to get practice in recognizing as well as distinguishing between positive and negative processes.

1. Make a list of positive processes you run in your life. Examples: 1) You were successful at planning a work project. It was completed successfully in a week as planned. 2) You are very good at listening and understanding people. 3) You have been successfully saving money to buy a new home. 4) You are good at having fun times with your family. For example, you surprise them by taking them all to a special theme park.

2. Make a list of negative processes you run in your life. Examples: 1) You decided that you wanted to incur no debt for the year and yet you incurred more debt by the end of the year. 2) You wanted to have a great evening out with your spouse, but instead you got irritated and you provoked an argument. 3) You were late for a business appointment and kept a customer waiting.

3. Make a list of positive processes you see that others are running.

4. Make a list of negative processes you see that others are running.

5. Write down some positive processes that you would like to implement in your life. Make a plan of how you would like to implement them and then start to implement them if you wish. This book contains ideas that will show you how to implement them.

CHAPTER 2

HAVING A POSITIVE ATTITUDE TOWARD GIVING

"The unexamined life is not worth living."
—Socrates

O ur attitude is key when it comes to being directors of the stage productions of our lives. If we have a positive attitude, we will have a positive production, thus a positive life. If we have a negative attitude, we will have a negative production, thus a negative life.

Likewise, each person also has a choice of one of two attitudes concerning giving. Those who have a positive attitude toward giving will run positive processes concerning giving and will positively process those who give. They will experience joy and fulfillment from all the gifts they receive due to all they give. Those who have a negative attitude toward giving will run negative processes concerning giving and will negatively process those who give. Their lives will be unfulfilling as a result of the absence of their giving.

An action of giving is an action that helps others have their dreams and aspirations come true. The more we give, the more we become a part of The Giving Zone. And since we live in a reciprocal universe, the more we give to others, the more our own dreams and aspirations come true. The Giving Zone – the zone of trust, love, prosperity, happiness, fun, and unity becomes our playground.

If it were an ideal world, we would all be able to give to the max, and correspondingly, we would all be able to receive to the max. All of us would be enjoying life in The Giving Zone. This would be the ultimate positive process. But our world is far from ideal. Most people have a degree of reluctance to give, and give at a level far beneath their capacity.

Why is this?

Much of this reluctance to give has to do with our particular programming. Just as a computer is programmed to automatically do a particular activity, we each have programs that have us automatically do a particular activity in our lives. We all have particular programs that determine how much we give in our lives.

> I remember as a young child growing up in Chicago that there was a kind of peer pressure among many boys. We all had a silent code of agreement, which we didn't really make verbally or consciously. It was so deeply buried in my mind that I didn't become aware of it until many years later.
>
> Our agreement was that we were to give as little to the teacher and other adults as possible. We decided to do as little school work as we could, to cooperate as little as possible, and to help as little as possible. It just wasn't cool to do school work or to give to others. This was a very negative process that had detrimental consequences.

This pattern is not uncommon. Many people in our society don't feel comfortable giving freely. Joel Haggar, an associate of mine, wrote about his own childhood programming, which was also to give as little as possible. The following passage became an impetus for me to write this book:

The real area that most of us need to be working on is our ability to truly give. The problem is not that we've been conditioned or programmed to only let a little in, it's that we've been conditioned and programmed to only let a little out – to only *give* as little as possible and get as much as we can.

Haggar continues:

> I looked at what my friends growing up were willing to give and it wasn't much of anything, but they were willing to steal, take advantage of, cheat, and vandalize. And guess who was ridiculed the most – people that added value to the community and school, and offered positive exchanges.
>
> ....I realized how much I had been programmed from children in school, and people I've worked with to give as little as possible and get as much as I can. I was in ... agreement with this mindset quite a bit of the time in my life....

Just like Joel, my programming also greatly limited me in my ability to give. And because of my particular programming to not give, I was in opposition to my family, particularly, my mother. She wanted me to cooperate by being helpful – doing chores, making my bed, etc. I rebelled because I felt it was "uncool" to give or to be cooperative.

This negative program had very negative and weakening effects on my life in my earlier years and definitely kept me from being in The Giving Zone.

A major part of our lives is concerned with *exchange*. At all times we are either reciprocating or holding back from reciprocating. When we give freely, we tend to have a lot to exchange, and then we are very powerful in our ability to reciprocate – a very positive process.

When we give freely and wholeheartedly, we each create a dynamic in which there is a great "flow" causing massive reciprocation that affects many people around us. Others are encouraged to give and this creates a ripple effect causing more and more people to give.

The opposite occurs when a person or group does not participate in the giving process. In the opposite way, many people can be affected negatively.

Haggar also writes that operating from this basis as a child virtually stopped the flow of reciprocation from occurring and this caused upsets.

What causes someone to be upset? A major cause of an upset is when you give something of value to someone and get nothing back in return. An upset can also come from the opposite behavior. You receive something of value from someone and give nothing back. These are both common negative processes.

This understanding has made a big difference in my life. I now see that it's important to give freely and to be willing to receive freely. Receiving freely is important because it gives others the opportunity to give.

If I'm upset in my life, it's often because I've given something of value and gotten nothing back, or because I've received something of value and given nothing back. It's that simple. When you see someone who is upset, that person quite possibly has either been giving and getting nothing back, or getting and giving nothing back. This explains why many parents can become so upset. They give and give to their children and the children give nothing back. Many parents wait hand and foot on their children. These children thus expect to be given everything and are trained not to have to give back. When the parents ask these children to give back by being responsible, doing chores, and being respectful, the children will often ignore their parents and continue to take and give nothing back.

What's worse is that these children often resent their parents and do not respect them. You may ask why this is so. It's because when you give to others and don't really expect them to give back, you can end up spoiling them. They *expect* you to give – and to give continually, without any need to reciprocate.

These children resent their parents because they know subconsciously that they owe their parents a lot for what they have been given. They work unknowingly to block out in their mind the obligations they owe. If they were to admit that they owe their parents, they would have to give a lot back to them. Instead of admitting they should give back, they turn their sense of obligation into resentment directed at their parents. Again, this is done unknowingly.

This explains why there are so many people who give so generously to people they are close to, but then they are routinely upset that these same people resent them. The way to prevent these upsets is to motivate the people you give to, including your children, to give back.

The other side of the equation is that we need to be sure to give back to people who have given us a great deal.

As I mentioned, as a boy, I was upset from being around other boys who held to a silent code of agreement that they would give as little to the teacher and other adults as possible. I believe that we all have a natural propensity to give. I remember that I had a desire to give, but as a result of the boys' negative influence, I greatly restrained my true desire to give. This made me upset – and so much so that it caused me to have negative behavior.

One of the things I regret is that this pattern contributed to my doing as little schoolwork as possible in grade school. What's worse is that as a young adult at the age of 18, I had a weak work ethic.

One of the young men who worked with me at a part-time job suggested that we do as little work as possible. I'm ashamed to say that for a couple of days I participated in this, getting by with time spent not working. It didn't feel right and I stopped it immediately. It was a very negative process.

Certainly my beginnings were not uncommon. I had to learn right from wrong by making lots of mistakes and correcting them.

It is also important to note that there are children who are taught from an early age to give freely. They are the very fortunate. There are also many examples of people who give without reservation in our society. They understand that the flow of life has much to do with giving.

One of the best recent examples of generosity was shown to us by the many heroes who acted to change lives when Hurricane Katrina hit New Orleans in 2005. This includes the rescue people, those who put people up in their homes, the millions who have given financial support, and those many other unsung heroes who have given their time in so many ways.

A relatively small number of people started to give without hesitation. Soon others followed suit and many more came through to help relieve the suffering of so many. This is an example of the essence of giving – people who stand up and decide to give freely. They inspire others who also stand up and decide to give freely. It repeats and repeats and builds until millions of people all over the world may get involved. We can call this "the flow of giving" – a very positive process.

It's natural to give of ourselves to others and be in The Giving Zone – the zone of helping others to realize their dreams and aspirations, which in turn forwards our dreams and aspirations to come true as well. Each of us has so much to offer. It is a great gift to be able to overcome any limitations and restraints that might stop us from giving freely of ourselves to help others.

CHAPTER 2 EXERCISE

This exercise can help you become aware of the attitudes about giving you developed early in your life. You will find that these attitudes have had a profound effect on your life.

1. Write down the attitudes that were in your family, school, religious organizations, peers, etc. about giving to others that you picked up from your childhood.

2. Organize the list into two categories – positive attitudes toward giving and negative attitudes toward giving.

3. Prioritize the lists in order of the attitudes you feel most affected you.

CHAPTER 3

BREAKING SILENT AGREEMENTS

*"Great spirits have always encountered
violent opposition from mediocre minds."*
—Albert Einstein

*I*n the second chapter, I mentioned a type of destructive group
behavior I was part of – a very negative process. The unspoken
mission of the silent group to which I belonged was to make sure
that boys did not cooperate with teachers and other adults and
did not give to others. We were directors of a stage production to
undermine the giving process.

I unknowingly bought into this destructive way of thinking
which prevented me from entering The Giving Zone. And it had
a profound negative effect on me – until I became aware of it and
let go of this destructive group think.

Alan Walter calls this silent code of agreement "tacit sabotage." *Tacit* means "unspoken." A major definition of *sabotage* is
"any underhanded effort to defeat or do harm to an endeavor."

---

*Tacit sabotage is an unspoken agreement to do something under-
handed that will defeat or do harm to an endeavor.*

Tacit sabotage pervades our society, affecting the workplace as well as the home.

Tacit agreements stop the flow of giving and receiving.

One such tacit agreement related to giving involves two or more people:

Their agreement is: "I won't give much if you won't give much."

This type of agreement destroys marriages, companies, and nations. As you will see in the following examples, one thing that all tacit sabotage agreements have in common is that they stop people or slow people down from being able to give.

> *One client of mine admired his father. His father had a belief that people who are wealthy are evil. The father was amongst many who had the agreement that wealthy people are evil. This is a cultural tacit agreement lasting generations that has negative consequences. In this case it's an unspoken rule that you have to have very little money to be part of this group.*
>
> *If one person starts accumulating money and others of this same mindset find out, that person will be heavily ridiculed, unless that person spends it recklessly on friends and quickly gets rid of it.*
>
> *My client who was part of this program turned into an adult. He found that he was always broke and didn't understand why. He unwittingly was operating from the belief he adopted from his father that wealthy people are evil.*
>
> **Each time he started to accumulate any money, he spent it or lost it because he didn't want to be evil. It was only until he worked on eliminating this destructive program, that he began to be able to succeed financially.**

Tacit sabotage in the workplace goes like this: A group of workers have a silent agreement not to work hard. Their unspoken rule is to do as little as possible. The silent pact is "I won't work hard if you won't work hard." This type of agreement destroys companies.

Typically, this behavior is so deeply embedded that if the boss hires a new person for the job who is an honest, capable hard worker, it won't be long before that person either conforms to the low level of production of the other workers or quits.

The reason for this is that when he comes to work the first day and works fully at the job, the other workers will sabotage him to get him down to their level. They begin to criticize him, threaten and ostracize.

The workers comments to him are "You know, you don't have to work so hard around here." "Do you think you are better than we are?" "You think you're so good." "You better watch out."

Three days later the new worker quits. He doesn't understand why "everyone hated him" at the job. The boss doesn't understand why the new capable recruit quit.

Salespeople can have this same type of agreement: One group of computer salespeople is given a small salary plus a commission bonus if they do well. This particular group forms a tacit agreement to do just enough to get by and keep their jobs.

A new salesperson is hired who has a strong work ethic. He wants to break all records, work long hours and do whatever it takes to succeed.

The other salespeople start to ridicule him, tell him he doesn't need to work so hard, and begin to make small threats.

He does not understand why the other salespeople are continually punishing him. He becomes upset, loses his ability to concentrate on the job and quits after a month. The group of salespeople won. They preserved their tacit agreement to do just enough to get by.

They celebrate the evening the salesperson quits by going out for a few beers.

This type of behavior is completely the opposite behavior of what it takes to be living in The Giving Zone. It is a very good example of The Destructive Zone – a zone of betrayal, hate, poverty, suffering, and fragmentation.

Another salesperson gets hired in this company. He is savvy to the tacit sabotage problem in the work world. He spots the hostility immediately when he shows up at work the first day.

He then meets with the boss, and makes the boss aware of the problem. He and the boss arrange that he will have a separate office across town to work in so he can be away from the other salespeople. He produces well and soon becomes a sales manager of another group of salespeople who do want to work. His positive processes cause him to be a very competent director of the successful stage production of his career.

One of the most vicious types of tacit sabotage agreements is when people in the workplace decide to gossip.

This is a tacit agreement to gossip. A person spreads malicious gossip about a co-worker and pretends it's the truth. The others in the office don't say anything. Their tacit agreement is: "I won't let anyone know you're spreading malicious gossip if you won't let anyone know I'm spreading malicious gossip."

Alan Walter says:

Tacit sabotage agreements are deadly.

Companies can be crippled or destroyed because of the problem of gossip and the accompanying problems that follow.

The author was a consultant to an insurance company in which the gossip about the agency manager could have damaged his career. One agent had spread a false accusation about the agency manager but the other agents didn't question his obvious distortion of truth. They tacitly agreed to not say a word as this false information rapidly spread its damage throughout the company.

The most aggravating part of this scenario is that the agents who heard this gossip didn't confront the perpetrator. They remained silent.

Their tacit agreement was, "I won't question what you are doing, if you won't question what I'm doing."

The agency manager was coached by the author on how to spot and handle tacit sabotage. He used a very effective communication tool to put an end to the gossip: An employee, Rick, told the agency manager that John, another employee, was spreading a rumor. The agency manager quickly arranged a meeting in which he confronted John for starting the rumor and Rick for spreading it. The rumor was immediately proven false. Through this upfront technique, the gossip problem in the insurance company quickly stopped.

Tacit agreements destroy many marriages.

A couple has serious problems. Neither of them is willing to talk about it. The tacit sabotage agreement of the couple is: "I won't look at what you're doing, if you won't look at what I'm doing." The other tacit sabotage agreement of this couple is: "I won't talk about it if you won't talk about it."

You cannot solve a marital problem without communication. The withholding of communication between spouses is very destructive to the marriage.

Inspect the different areas of your life and see if you can spot the tacit sabotage agreements you are operating in as well as the tacit sabotage agreements other people you relate to are operating in.

In order to give freely and reside in The Giving Zone we must be able to break free from these tacit agreements.

Tacit sabotage is a great hindrance to giving – undermining generosity, and doing harm. These agreements are so hidden that the vast majority of people are completely unaware that they exist.

It is generally not easy to break these agreements. But if you start to become aware of them, you can begin the process of disagreeing, discussing them and letting go of them. Coaching and training from someone experienced in the area can help you make positive changes.

To embark on the journey of breaking these silent codes of conduct is one of the greatest acts of giving to others as well as to yourself. It is a quintessential positive process and, it will enable you to become a leading participant in The Giving Zone.

CHAPTER 3 EXERCISE

The purpose of this exercise is to begin to become aware of tacit (silent) agreements we may have and how they affect us and the people with whom we come in contact.

1. Do you have a silent code of agreement in your marriage, family, career, etc. that involves a tacit agreement not to talk about it? Write it down.

2. If so, write how it has affected you and the others involved. Think of as many ways as you can that it has affected you and those involved.

3. Write down some ideas of how you could solve this tacit agreement. Keep writing these ideas until you have a realization of something important that gives you deeper insight.

4. Repeat 1. to 3. over and over until you've had a significant shift in your awareness.

CHAPTER 4

BEING YOURSELF

"You must be the change you wish to see in the world."
—Mahatma Gandhi

A great gift for others and for yourself is simply to be the unique person that you are. The more you are yourself, the more unique you are. The more you stand out as yourself, the greater the contribution you can make. This is because when you are being fully yourself, you have little or no restraint on your life force, and your personal power can shine.

As the director of your life, in being yourself, you create a unique stage production in life, not a carbon copy of someone else's stage production. Being who you are is a vital, positive process. If you are not being who you are, it is very possible that you have conformed unwittingly to others – a very negative process.

It is completely natural to give. The more you are yourself, the more you give. Being fully "you," there is no restraint on giving. The Giving Zone is filled with people who are very strongly themselves. They are unique individuals. Each is one of a kind.

Many people are programmed to believe it's not OK to be yourself. They feel that they have to be someone else. Or that it's selfish to be yourself. Perhaps they believe it's not safe to be yourself. Or they believe they can be more successful by being someone else.

In my childhood and early adulthood, I was basically not myself. I was a very conformed individual. For example, I did whatever I was told in school for fear of being punished. I saw the consequences of what happened to certain children who didn't conform to what was expected.

This taught me to please others, particularly authority. I did what I was told. I followed "the school program" and frequently it wasn't what I wanted to do. The consequences were that I was not myself, and thus I had little creativity, freedom, or happiness. I learned to do what I didn't want to do. I put on different identities or cloaks to survive. One of my identities was the "pleasing school child." Another was "the conformed child."

I was so busy being what others wanted me to be, the essence or "spirit" of me was absent. Being absent, I had little to give, and for the most part I was not a participant in The Giving Zone.

Fortunately, I decided early in life to get some help. I felt that something was wrong. I received consulting and training help. As a result, I became much more myself – with the accompanying freedom, creativity, and happiness – and with a much greater capacity to give.

The following humorous story illustrates what our lives are like when we are not ourselves:

At a popular zoo, the main attraction was a gorilla. One day the gorilla died. Ticket sales dropped to almost zero.

The zookeeper didn't know what to do. He was going bankrupt. In the meantime, there was an unemployed man with a gorilla suit. He was very desperate for work. He went to the zookeeper and pleaded for a job. He said, "Put me in the cage; I'll put on the gorilla suit and I'll even be better than the real gorilla you had before. You don't even have to pay me for two weeks."

The zookeeper thought the guy was nuts, but since he was equally desperate he decided to give the guy a chance.

The next day the man was put in the cage. He put on the gorilla suit. He started to jump all over the cage. He was fantastic as a gorilla. People started to come back to the zoo and ticket sales started to soar.

Ticket sales records were being broken as the gorilla started swinging back and forth higher and higher in the cage. Each day he'd swing higher and higher, until finally one day he swung so high, he flew into the lion's cage.

He was lying on his back and a huge lion leaped toward him. He was terrified for his life as he smelled the breath of the lion upon him. He yelled, "Please don't eat me," and the lion whispered in his ear, "Don't worry, I rented my costume too."

The moral of this story is: *Be yourself.* It is one of the greatest gifts you can give to yourself, as well as to others, because everyone will benefit when you are real –"yourself" rather than someone else.

Most people wear identities or cloaks to keep from being themselves. They live lives of seeking approval or pleasing others rather than being who they truly are. They sell themselves away to others rather than being true to themselves. They have no idea of the real identity, "the real me."

Being "the real me" puts you on the correct pathway in life. The more you are yourself, the more successful, giving, and happy you will become.

It is especially important to be "the real me" for the following reason: If we decide not to be "the real me," others will run our lives for us.

When we are not being who we are, there is an empty space or vacuum that opens up for others to enter and occupy the space of "the real me." Either we are in charge of our own lives, or others are in charge.

The more we are ourselves, the happier we are. This is because being ourselves means that we are in charge of our lives. This is freedom. When we are not ourselves, automatically others are running our lives. This is a major cause of unhappiness and will take us out of The Giving Zone.

The more you are yourself, the more you express your uniqueness and the greater the contribution you will make to others. One of the most unique and giving individuals of all time is Oprah Winfrey. She is one of a kind and there is no one like her. Another unique person was one of the most generous individuals of all time. That was Mother Theresa. These two women decided to be true to themselves, with extraordinary results.

A major aspect of being who you are is discovering what you really want to do in life. Each of us has a special life purpose. When we discover what we truly want to do at the deepest level possible, we have discovered our life purpose. This becomes a major source of endless fulfillment and happiness.

Our life purpose is always about making a contribution that will benefit others. Those people who make the biggest contributions are working in the direction of their life purpose.

Alan Walter, author of *The Secrets to Increasing Your Power, Wealth and Happiness,* says:

Your dream is the conduit to your power.

The word *dream* means "a strongly desired goal or purpose." When individuals are living their dream, their lives have great meaning with the potential for great happiness.

To help find out who you are ask yourself, "Who am I?" Take some time to repeat this question over, and over again, writing the answers as they come to you.

The quest for the discovery of "the real me" is perhaps the most worthy adventure of our lives. For most people, there are many layers to be peeled off in the discovery of "the real me." Many of the outer layers are false identities we have taken on to adapt and survive such as "pleaser," "accommodator," and "victim." False identities cause us to not be ourselves, bringing about inner conflicts and unfavorable results.

The discovery and actualization of becoming oneself is a major part of the gift of life and one of the most positive processes that there is. The more you are yourself, the more you will naturally give to others, and the more successful and happy you will be, living in The Giving Zone.

CHAPTER 4 EXERCISE

The purpose of this exercise is to help discover qualities that are uniquely "you" and to implement those qualities in your life.

1. Write down some positive activities that you really enjoy doing.

2. Take each positive activity and write down something that is uniquely you when you are doing that activity.

3. Take each quality that is uniquely you in those activities and write down how you can implement more of that unique quality in your life.

CHAPTER 5

BEING IN A HIGH MOOD

"The future is something which everyone reaches at the rate of 60 minutes an hour, whatever he does, whoever he is."
—C.S. Lewis

*H*ave you ever been around someone who was continually in a low mood? Perhaps that person was depressed, afraid, sad, or angry. A person in a low mood can drag other people down. If you are continually around someone in a low mood, for example, someone who is depressed, it can be like having a huge weight around your neck. Of course it works the other way too. If I am continually in a low mood, I will tend to pull down the people around me. It is important to understand that virtually all of us experience low moods at times. This is normal. The problem occurs from continually being stuck in a low mood.

A continual low mood is a negative process. For directors of life, it will cause poor stage productions. When we are predominantly in a high mood, we are positively processing, and as directors of our lives, we will create winning performances.

When I use the term *mood*, I'm talking about emotions and feelings as well as one's state of mind.

How does it feel to be around someone in a high mood?

To our delight, a person with enthusiasm and joy will tend to boost everyone up around them. It's a great gift to offer others a high mood when you are with them.

If we are predominantly in a low mood, it is very difficult to give much to others – and we will not be living our lives in The Giving Zone. If we are predominantly in a high mood, it is much easier to give to others and enter The Giving Zone.

Earlier in my marriage, I had the bad habit of being in a low mood for hours at a time. I was often gloomy, irritated, or angry. It had a negative effect on my wife. It would bring her mood down, too. She would feel unhappy. I was not giving – I was taking. It had the effect of sapping her energy.

When I was in a positive mood, it would bring her mood up. I was giving and it replenished her energy.

In a seminar I learned that when I'm around others and I'm in a low mood for hours at a time, it actually ties up their attention and sabotages them.

This awareness was a wake-up call for me, and I soon made a conscious effort to work hard on self-improvement and raise my mood level. As a consequence, the quality of our marriage greatly improved and overall the quality of my life greatly improved.

There are exceptions of when it is OK to be in a low mood. If we are around people in a low mood and we are in a high mood, they are likely to feel uncomfortable. This is because we are not relating to them. They may be miserable while we are feeling that everything is going great.

When this happens, we need to use the skill of bridging moods. This involves lowering your mood and then relating to the experience of the other person. Then you gradually raise your mood in the conversation to help lift that person's mood.

A good example is when we attend a funeral. People in grief are feeling emotional pain. If we express cheerfulness to them, it will probably make them feel worse. If on the other hand, we match our mood to the level of their mood – in this case grief – we will be relating to them. For example, we say in the mood level of grief, "I'm so sorry for your loss." This will connect us. Then we can raise our mood a bit to help them raise theirs.

Susan walks into a restaurant and notices that her waitress looks upset. The waitress is overworked and is having to take care of too many tables. Susan lowers her mood to that of the waitress and says, "It looks like it's been a tough day." The waitress, hearing her words, snaps out of her low mood, smiles and says, "Yes it has been one of those days. Thank you for noticing."

Then Susan continues to converse with the waitress, creates a nice connection, gradually helping to brighten her mood even more.

Emotions involve a very special language. It is the language of the spirit. For example, when we are in a low mood, we tend to be low-spirited. When we are in a high mood, we tend to be high spirited.

A key definition of *spirit* is: "That which is traditionally believed to be the vital principle or animating force within all living beings."

When people are in a high mood they are quite animated and alive. They are expressing more of the spirit that they are. And the higher the mood, the higher the truth that person has. When we operate our lives by being truthful, we tend to feel good about ourselves.

When we feel good about ourselves, we tend to have a high mood.

When people go around in life with a low mood, it generally means that they are not being truthful about something. It could be that they are not being truthful about something concerning themselves or it could be that they are not being truthful about something concerning others.

An example is Bob who is feeling low because he thinks

he is not worthy of the awards he's getting at work. Even though he has been doing a very good job, his feelings of unworthiness dominate him. These feelings of unworthiness are not based on truth. No matter how well he does at work, he feels he's not good enough. This belief that he's not good enough is not true.

On the other hand, Jill is feeling very enthusiastic because she helped a customer resolve his financial problems. She is very truthful in how she does her work. The customer is now dealing with his finances more accurately and will make his payments on time. Jill has operated at a high level of truth and feels great inside.

At work it is nearly always necessary for us to have a high mood in order to do our job.

A low mood will tend to undermine our work.

When we are in a low mood, we tend to not be happy about what whatever activity we are doing. When we are in a high mood we tend to be happy about whatever activity we are doing. Another way of understanding this concept is that when we are in a low mood, we are usually not in alignment with what we are doing. When we are in a high mood, we tend to be in alignment with what we are doing.

Rob is a salesperson who has a client to see first thing in the morning. Rob's mood is very low. He does not like his job and he disagrees with some of what he considers dishonest sales tactics used by his company.

Rob is feeling depressed and would rather not have to talk with the client. He talks to his client in a depressed mood. The client feels uncomfortable with him. He feels dragged down by Rob's low mood. He walks out the door without buying.

Rob actually feels a little relieved because if he had

made the sale, he would have been dishonest, due to the questionable sales tactics of his company. Being basically good, he doesn't want to be dishonest. His low mood is an expression of his not being in alignment with what he is doing.

Another example illustrates again how a low mood can affect our lives:

Glenda manufactures handmade musical instruments. On one particular day, she is feeling very unhappy about a family problem. She notices after awhile that she has made a couple of mistakes that she rarely does. This is because she can't concentrate well from feeling so unhappy. She would rather not be at work. Her low mood is an expression of not being in alignment with what she is doing.

Another skill that relatively few people possess is the ability to change one's moods at will. A person who has this skill actually can decide to have a higher mood or lower mood, choose it, and move into it.

This is not an easy task and takes quite a bit of training and practice. However, most of us already know how to change our mood on the spot in some situations. This is nearly always done unconsciously.

An example is Joan who is in a fierce argument with her husband and is feeling very angry with him. Suddenly, her neighbors stop by unexpectedly. When she lets them in the door, she puts a smile on her face and after a minute of visiting, she forgets the upset, and her mood lifts.

If we learn to change our moods consciously for the particular situation at hand, we have a superior skill and a vastly improved life.

In summary, not only are we giving people a special gift when we are around them in a high mood, but we can also give people the gift of helping them raise their mood.

The ability to understand and work with yours and others' moods is one of the most important abilities you can have to further your life and the lives of others. Others will benefit from your ability to be predominantly in a positive mood and to be able to help lift up their moods. This will result in your being a tremendous inspiration to those around you, a more effective leader, and a better friend.

A positive mood is nearly a prerequisite for being in The Giving Zone. It's hard to be depressed and give at the same time. For example, if we take depressed people and inspire them to do volunteer work, in the process of giving, their mood will rise significantly. This is a powerful key for helping others. Inspire them to give. They will feel better and begin to reside in The Giving Zone. This will result in the perpetual effect of people helping people helping people.

If you want to learn to become proficient with handling your moods, it is recommended that you find seminars, classes, and personal coaching for this purpose. Gain this knowledge and skill, and you will contribute greatly to the success and happiness of yourself as well as of other people in your life.

CHAPTER 5 EXERCISE

The purpose of this exercise is to help you become more aware of the high moods you experience and to be able to increase how often you experience high moods.

1. Select a high mood – such as joy, enthusiasm, or excitement – that you would like to express more of in your life.

2. Select one person connected to you in your career, marriage, family, friendships, etc. with whom you would like to express more of that mood.

3. Write down the things that are likely to happen if you were to express more of that mood with that person. Write what's likely to happen until you've had a realization of something important that gives you deeper insight.

4. Repeat 1. to 3. until you've had a significant shift in your awareness.

CHAPTER 6

EMBRACING FAILURE

*"I don't believe in failure.
It's not failure if you enjoyed the process."*
—Oprah Winfrey

Give the people in your life the gift of embracing failure. This allows others to make mistakes and experience failure. Of course before you can do this, you first need to give the same gift to yourself.

Failure is defined as "the condition or fact of not achieving the desired end or ends." Every time we learn something new, we continually have the experience of not achieving the desired end or result. This is because we are not competent yet in that area. When we first start out, we don't get it right; we correct our action and do it again, repeating this process over and over until we get it right.

Robert Kiyosaki, author of the best-selling *Rich Dad Poor Dad* points out that we are taught in school not to make mistakes. However, he stresses that the process of learning comes only by making mistakes. The problem is, if it's not OK to make mistakes, we don't try.

William Glasser in *Schools Without Failure* writes about the effects of giving children grades. The grading system is based on being punished for making mistakes. The result is that millions of children become adults who experience paralysis when it comes to taking action. They cannot take action because of fear of doing it wrong. They are trained to be perfectionists. The problem with trying to be a perfectionist is that you cannot make any mistakes. And the only way you won't make mistakes is if you don't take action.

People conditioned not to make mistakes and not to fail can suffer tremendous emotional pain and loss of self-esteem. Each time a mistake is made, they beat themselves up inside. This is a destructive negative process and creates unhappy stage productions in life.

Rudolf Dreikurs, MD, author of *Children the Challenge*, taught that we tend to be harder on ourselves than any enemy could be. No wonder. We grew up with the predominant pattern of having been punished while in the process of learning and doing.

The external program of phrases such as "You are stupid; you're a failure," internalize into "I'm stupid; I'm a failure."

Alan Walter says:

Perfectionism is the ultimate sabotage.

We sabotage the learning process and future success of children by teaching them that they shouldn't make mistakes. They have to get it perfect. This message contributes to many children living failed lives as adults.

How does a baby learn to walk? It is through falling. A baby falls hundreds if not thousands of times on its way to walking. As a parent we allow the baby to fall. We are encouraging and nurturing. This is the opposite of how most people treat themselves and others pertaining to falling and making mistakes.

To come into The Giving Zone, it is required that we allow ourselves and others to make mistakes and experience failure as a key not only to the learning process, but also to the giving process.

Criticizing people for making mistakes and failing has the effect of putting them in a prison. It is like a mental prison with heavy steel bars. As an inmate of such a prison, we cannot act; we are confined. If we were to act, we would make mistakes and risk failure – a forbidden crime.

To live in The Giving Zone, we need to allow all people including ourselves to make plenty of mistakes on the way to success. After all, we cannot give to others without the possibility of making mistakes in the process of giving itself.

How does an inventor succeed? It is through the process of failing over and over until success is achieved. Thomas Edison completed 10,000 attempts at making a light bulb until he succeeded.

> *About 27 years ago I became an intermediate skier fairly quickly. Why? Because I'd get on the skis and fall. I'd get back on the skis and fall again. I repeated this process and got better and better. I did not consider it bad or a mistake to fall. I knew it was part of the process of learning.*

Abraham Lincoln said, "My great concern is not if you have failed, it is if you are content with your failure." He is saying that since we all fail, we can choose to have a positive attitude toward it. This is not an easy lesson. Personally it has taken me many years just to begin to learn this lesson. I heard his quote years ago and certainly didn't feel content with some major failures I'd experienced, until years later.

In my earlier years because my attention was largely on myself, and on what I could get, I experienced a great deal of failure. Once I shifted my focus from selfishness to giving, I was content with my previous failures because of the priceless lessons I learned. The basic lesson is: When I tend to be selfish, I will fail. When I tend to be giving, I experience results that lead to success – and I will be living in The Giving Zone.

David C. Johnson, accomplished in the world of video production, goes by the motto, "Make mistakes as fast as you can!"

Thomas Watson, a past president of IBM said, "The formula for success is to double your failure rate." So give yourself activities that allow you to learn twice as fast because you have twice as many chances of getting it wrong and failing, and you'll be on your way to getting it right, and succeeding.

Elbert Hubert said, "Failure is a man who has blundered, but is not able to cash in on the experience."

The truth is, failure is a major part of the formula for success. Many of the most successful people in the world experienced massive failure.

Thomas Edison was thrown out of school in the early grades because the teachers thought he was too stupid to do the work. Clement Stone, a billionaire insurance legend and founder of *Success* magazine, was a high-school dropout.

Bob Dylan, famous singer and songwriter, had an opportunity when he was in high school to perform in front of his peers. When he played his music, he was literally booed off the stage. This was a major failure at this impressionable time in his life. Did he give up? No. He kept going.

A key part of the formula for success of these great people is the embracing of failure. This acceptance of failure is an essential ingredient for entrance into The Giving Zone. At the heart of giving is tolerance and compassion. We all need to cultivate tolerance and compassion for the mistakes and failures of others and ourselves. It is core to the giving process and it will help us be great directors on the stage of our lives.

Learn to embrace failure, and help others embrace failure. The freedom generated from this gift will throw off the many shackles that limit us from learning, doing, and giving. You will help heal many others who suffer because they haven't learned to understand and embrace failure.

CHAPTER 6 EXERCISE

1. Write down a failure or a big mistake you made in your life.

2. Write down the things that you learned (your learning lessons) from that failure or big mistake.

3. If you have not learned one or more of those lessons yet, write down what you could do now to learn those lessons.

4. Repeat 1. to 3. over and over until you've had a realization of something important that gives you deeper awareness.

CHAPTER 7

BEING HONEST

"Only the honest person is a true asset to his company, his friends, his family and himself.... We are not happy unless we are honest. This is true of all people. The honest person is the most successful person."
—Alan C. Walter

This is a favorite chapter of mine because honesty is by far one of the most important qualities connected to giving. It is perpetual in its effects. One act of honesty will impel other acts of honesty ad infinitum, having the potential to improve the entire world. One lie will impel other lies ad infinitum, having the potential to adversely affect many people. Honesty is a supreme positive process.

The definition of *honest* is: "not lying, cheating, stealing, exaggerating, omitting some of the truth, pretending, making false promises, or taking unfair advantage of; honorable; truthful; trustworthy."

A lack of honesty creates false giving – the giving of false hopes, false purposes, false promises, false dreams, and false love.

When people are truly honest, they are carriers of the rare gift of character. Truly honest individuals are a "walking gift" because they influence the lives of many by expressing integrity. The truly honest person takes actions that lead to success, prosperity, and happiness.

An act of dishonesty is an act of taking. It is the robbing of someone's love, well-being, trust, spirit, commitment, time, energy, effort, money, property, etc.

An act of honesty is an act of giving. It is the giving to someone's love, well-being, trust, spirit, commitment, time, energy, effort, money, property, etc.

Therefore, honesty is a major key to being part of The Giving Zone.

There are relatively few people who are completely honest. Why is this? What is behind people deciding to be dishonest? I believe the major cause is *ignorance. Ignorance* may be defined as "the condition of being uneducated, unaware, or uninformed."

This ignorance causes destructive behavior. It is the cementing of a dishonest person with a dishonest act. It is the creation of an allegiance between a dishonest person and a dishonest act.

The core of this destructive behavior is that dishonest people will reason in their minds that it is all right to be dishonest.

A businessperson overcharges a customer and makes it right by thinking, "He'll never know."

A job applicant falsifies resume statements and rationalizes it in her mind, "Everyone else does it, so why shouldn't I?"

A man cheats on his wife; he rationalizes it by thinking, "She hurt me – she's getting what she deserves."

This type of reasoning causes ruined lives. It is often unconsciously activated and is deeply entrenched in the mind. It is pervasive.

Each act of rationalization – each act of dishonesty – sets us adrift. It is perpetual in its effects.

Each act of dishonesty is an auctioning off of a bit of our soul. The bidder is the willing participant who will buy our act of dishonesty and will reap its harmful consequences.

The key is to be completely honest; the effects will be of heroic proportions. You will profoundly affect the lives of many. You will be able to greet the "real boss" that you see in the mirror each morning with deep respect. You will have a clear conscience, peace of mind, and a great capacity to laugh, and have fun.

A dilemma is that nearly all people, if you ask them, will tell you that they are honest. Even a criminal who steals will often feel that he is honest because "society doesn't give him what he deserves." He may feel that he is taking what is justly his. He may even justify that what he is doing is for the good.

Dishonest people attract other dishonest people into their lives. Their lives consequently become saturated with a copious harvest of dishonesty directed toward them.

A person who is very honest will attract honest people as their friends and associates. Being part of a group of honest people will practically guarantee a winning life – a life of truth, integrity, strong character, wholeness, and fulfillment.

The degree to which you are truthful in all phases of your life is the foundation of your character. Truth is the compass of life; any exaggeration, false claim, failure to keep your word, or violation of the Golden Rule will diminish your character and put you in the wrong time and the wrong place, moving you in the direction of failure. Compromising of truth paralyzes faith.

The ability to be influential for the good is dependent on complete unadulterated truthfulness.

Unfortunately many people would disagree with this. They may believe that you can't win in life if you are truthful and of strong character. It is true that dishonest people can succeed. However, their success is built on a foundation of lies that eventually catches up with them and will inevitably destroy their success. Dishonest people have to juggle from one lie to the next, always looking over their shoulder to try to keep from getting caught. Eventually, their lies will bury them and the weak foundation of their supposed success will crumble.

Quite a few people think that white lies are OK. This is not the case. Honesty is like pregnancy. Either you are honest or you are not.

The following saying from the Talmud will not excuse a lie of any size:

"A half truth is a full lie."

Very honest people will not tolerate even slight dishonesty. They understand that even a slight lie could pull someone off course. For example, if I were late and missed a major appointment, I ended up in the wrong time and the wrong place. I could have missed the job opportunity of a lifetime.

When people lie to each other, it also puts them in the wrong time and the wrong place.

John gets fired because he gets caught for greatly overcharging customers. Now he is without a job, walking the streets for many months looking for work. The other shoe drops when the company he worked for presses charges and he is given a six-month sentence. A major wrong time and wrong place for John is jail.

It takes courage to be willing to locate our personal areas of dishonesty. Most people would rather blame others and not look at themselves.

You might ask, how do I discover the areas of dishonesty I

may have? One way to locate your dishonesties is to look at the results you are achieving in life.

The results you receive in your life reflect the degree of honesty you have. It is very simple. If you are truly winning in a particular area of your life, it means that you have honesty in that area of your life and you are winning in a way that is good for all concerned. It is not the type of winning which is at the expense of others. It is the type of winning where everyone benefits. This is implied in the definition of honesty. If a person wins at the expense of others, that person is operating at a level of dishonesty.

> *Paul is a middle manager with a fairly high salary. Yet, he is complaining that he is always broke and doesn't have money for many of the things he needs and wants. Since he is losing in the area of money, it means that he has dishonesties connected to money.*
>
> *In looking into Paul's finances, you find that he has several dishonesties. He has numerous current debts he promised to pay and yet he has not paid them. He is two years behind in his taxes. Also Paul has seven credit cards that are maxed out, and he declared bankruptcy only three years ago. When he declared bankruptcy, he had quite a few debts that he had promised to pay but he didn't pay them.*
>
> *No wonder he is broke. A deeper way to look at Paul's problem is to understand that he has been getting back what he has been giving. This is what Napoleon Hill calls **The Law of Reciprocation.***
>
> *Many people have suffered because he has not paid his debts. For example, his in-laws experienced a great financial loss when they lent him funds that came out of their retirement money. He also borrowed money from his best friend to start a business. Because Paul didn't pay it back, his friend's home was foreclosed.*
>
> ***"What you sow is what you reap." He has planted the seeds of making other people broke and thus he has reaped being broke himself.***

Ted is devastated that his wife left him and that she is filing for divorce. Ted has a history of troubled relationships. He has several dishonesties connected to his current marriage. On business trips he was unfaithful to her. He also promised her that he would be available for the children to attend soccer games, school activities, birthday parties, and vacations. He did not keep his word on these promises. He also would not communicate with his wife. He was not willing to discuss matters of importance. Thus, he had shunned his wife.

Again The Law of Reciprocation took place. He rejected her throughout the marriage. Therefore he received rejection back – his wife serving him divorce papers.

One of the challenges you may face if you are very honest is that people who are dishonest will try to get you to compromise your honesty.

"Look, everyone does it."

"Just do it this time; it won't make any difference."

"No one will find out."

"You'll never be successful because you are too honest."

It takes strength of character to hold to one's position on being honest. It is a major test in one's life. However, the rewards are many for the person who remains honest – a bright and untarnished future of success and happiness.

There are two categories of honesty. We have been referring mostly to being honest with others. The other type of honesty has to do with being honest to yourself. Do you do what you promise to yourself? Do you complete the plans you have for the day? Do you go to the gym and work out when you promised? Do you give yourself the day at the beach or a special outing with the family?

There was a time in my life in which I was more honest with others than I was with myself. I was careful to keep my word to others. But, if I made a promise to myself to get something done, I didn't consider it so important. I thought that being honest meant keeping your word to others, but that it wasn't so essential to keep my word to myself when it came to accomplishing personal goals. These personal goals included anything from not saving as much money as I promised myself to not taking time for myself to relax and play. There were negative consequences for not honoring my personal goals –physical stress; falling behind financially; and because I did not take time for myself, work became a grind.

Honesty has a fun-filled side. We need to keep our word about the fun things we want to do in our lives.

I plan fun activities in my life in order to have a balanced life. Last night I went to a professional basketball game with a friend. A couple of days ago, my wife and I went to a movie. My wife and I take vacations; we frequently dance. We love to take walks and hike. We go to plays and concerts. If I plan to schedule fun things in my life and I don't do them, I consider it an act of dishonesty. After all, it's not keeping my word.

Keeping our word to ourselves is very important. If we don't keep our word to ourselves, how trustworthy are we going to be in keeping our word to others?

Honesty has to do with doing what we say we are going to do, whether it is work-related or play-related. It is about keeping our word – one of our most valuable possessions.

Those who do not value their word nor keep their word have very dismal and empty lives. Those who cherish and keep their word have full lives and are amply rewarded. They are the heroes in our world.

Honesty is the most important quality in building your character. When you are very honest, you are a great model for others. You are a gift for those you touch. You are part of a select group of people who enjoy the many benefits of living in The Giving Zone.

CHAPTER 7 EXERCISES

EXERCISE ONE

1. Make a list of areas of your life where you are very honest.

2. Take one item from that list and write down how this honesty affects you and others. Write answers to this question until you've had a realization of something important that gives you a deeper insight.

3. Repeat 2. to 3. until you've had a significant shift in your awareness about honesty.

EXERCISE TWO

1. Make a list of areas of your life where you feel you need to be more honest.

2. Take one item from that list and write down how you could be more honest in that area.

3. What are the different ways this increased honesty would affect yourself and others? Write answers to this question until you've had a realization of something important that gives you a deeper insight.

4. Repeat 2. to 3. over and over until you've had a good shift in awareness.

CHAPTER 8

BEING STRAIGHTFORWARD

*"Who is more foolish, the child afraid of the dark
or the man afraid of the light?"*
—Maurice Freehull

*I*n this chapter let's discuss a quality related to giving having to
do with emotional courage and trustworthiness. It takes courage
to be up front with people. Straightforwardness also creates trust.
Most people are not straightforward in their communication. They
may be afraid of hurting someone's feelings, displeasing others, or
having others disapprove of them.

There are negative consequences that come from not being
straightforward with others. One major consequence is that it acts
to sabotage relationships.

*People get hurt because truth that is needed to be
known is withheld.*

Straightforwardness is a strong part of honesty and therefore
it is an essential trait needed to enter The Giving Zone.

Have you ever been in a situation where someone needs to tell
you something of a critical nature about you, but instead, that
person talks behind your back? You find out about that person's

complaint from someone else. The information inevitably is distorted, and, what's worse, an entire group has become privy to what has turned into malicious gossip.

Strong is the person who tells you straight up what is going on instead of going behind your back. Gossip is one of what Napoleon Hill calls the "seven deadly sins." Gossip ruins businesses and it ruins marriages.

Gossip is a vicious addiction that many people depend on for entertainment in their life. You frequently hear in the office, "let's get the latest gossip," and several people crowd around the water cooler.

> *Bill says to Judy, "Do you know what I heard Susie is doing?" And with a few people adding their comments, lies permeate throughout the office. Later that day, Susie is mortified by the gossip that a supposed friend relays back to her.*

An honest person, a person of character, would not pass the gossip along the chain.

There is a quick cure for gossip:

> *Bill says to Judy, "Do you know what I heard Susie is doing?" Judy hears Bill's story. She then takes Bill assertively by the arm over to Susie's office. Judy says to Bill, "Now tell Susie what you just told me."*

This will stop the spread of gossip immediately. Gossip only continues with willing participants. Recognize the evil of gossip and put a stop to it. Gossip's only purpose is to undermine and destroy people's lives.

It takes emotional courage to be truthful to someone or to a group when there are challenging circumstances. And, we may risk ridicule and disapproval. On the other hand, if we do not take a stand for the truth, we will likely commit harm to others as well as to ourselves.

To not be straightforward is destructive to the giving process. It undermines our actions as well as the actions of others. It shuts us out of The Giving Zone.

There are times that we need to share something with another that is of a sensitive nature. We may resist because we don't want to hurt the other person's feelings. However, we often will end up hurting the other person more because we don't share the whole truth.

Many years ago when I was in high school, I had a friend who talked too much. He was the type of person who could be on the phone and talk nonstop for what seemed like 15 or 20 minutes. During this incessant talking he would not show any interest in the person on the other end of the line. People were very irritated with this but didn't tell him. He kept losing friends because rather than tell him he talked too much, they would simply disappear from his life.

One day I told him about his problem. I shared in a very compassionate way that he talked more than he needed to. He thanked me and said that I was the only person who had told him about his problem. I felt that he was saying that I was the only one who cared enough to tell him the truth, and therefore, I was the one person who was truly being a friend.

It is important to communicate such sensitive information with compassion. There are creative ways to tell someone the truth and minimize the possible hurt.

Carol needs to tell her friend Jennifer about an annoying habit that Jennifer has. Carol has put off telling Jennifer because she doesn't want to embarrass her or hurt her feelings. Jennifer has the habit of being very critical of nearly everybody. When Jennifer is around Carol's friends, she tends to be quite critical of them. These friends complain to Carol.

Carol finally summons the courage to tell Jennifer, but does so in a compassionate way. She says, "Jennifer, I have something to share with you and I've been very hesitant and afraid, because I don't want to hurt your feelings. You are such a dear friend. But you should know that you can be quite critical at times. Some of my friends have been telling me that it bothers them. You are probably thinking that you are helping by telling them they need to do things better, but what they really like to hear is words of encouragement. I just thought it was important for you to know."

Not being straightforward in our communications brings about deception, hatred and disconnection in our relationships.

Being straightforward in our communications brings about trust, connection and closeness. Straightforwardness is a character trait that brings about love.

It's always helpful if you can to take time to plan how you will communicate something that's not favorable. Your tone, your attitude and your wording can go a long way in moderating the effects of your communication. Many people who are masterful in communication will use humor when telling another person what's on their mind.

Bill has been wanting to tell his employee Mark that he needs to stop interrupting customers when he is talking with them. One morning Bill catches Mark interrupting a customer for the third time in a few minutes. He takes Mark to the side and privately says, "Ease up. I know you played linebacker in high school, but if you keep tackling the customer by interrupting him, we'll need to give him a helmet."

When you can communicate in a straightforward manner to the people in your life, you will be offering a great gift and be a great friend. They will have someone they can trust and they will be able to count on you as a true ally in The Giving Zone. You will be able to direct award-winning stage productions in your life.

CHAPTER 8 EXERCISE

1. Is there anyone in your life with whom it would be helpful to be more straightforward?

2. How could you be more straightforward with that person?

3. What would be the consequences (results)? List the consequences until you've come to a realization of something important that gives you a deeper understanding.

4. Repeat 1. to 3. over and over until you've had a genuine shift in awareness.

CHAPTER 9

GAINING KNOWLEDGE TO GET BETTER

*"We can't become what we need to be
by remaining what we are."*
—Oprah Winfrey

The gift of learning and getting better and helping others learn and get better involves one of the most important aspects of giving. It has to do with the seeking of knowledge, and using that knowledge towards getting better in important areas of our lives. This is a fun process that makes life an exciting adventure. A life without self-betterment is a stagnant life. We have much less to offer others as well as to ourselves. The key to getting better is continuously gaining new knowledge.

This is primarily the seeking of new knowledge for the purpose of learning how to achieve our dreams and aspirations.

The gaining of this new knowledge sets us upon a journey, the adventure of living. A life of no new knowledge sets us upon no journey, no adventure, and little hope.

New knowledge gives us new life and happiness. No new knowledge gives us no life and emptiness.
Those who continually seek new knowledge are growing and thus more alive. Those who do not seek new knowledge are stagnant and barely living their lives.

Have you ever been around people who don't want to learn anything new, who never want to get better in any area of life? It is likely to be boring to be around these people. Everything is the same every day – typically an intense dislike of their job, lots of complaining, and a long evening of repetition of the same TV shows.

Happiness can be nearly equated with the pursuit of continually learning, improving, and achieving one's dreams and aspirations. Unhappiness, especially depression, can be nearly equated with *not* working toward getting better and therefore *not* achieving ones dreams and aspirations.

Children playing and having fun are continually in the process of discovery and self-betterment. This is a joyful process for them that creates a joyful world. When we (as adults) get down on our hands and knees and enter their world to play with them, we experience this tremendous joy too.

Those who do not strive to learn, improve, and grow will often hold not only themselves back, but hold others back as well. People who are striving to learn, improve, and grow spark others to strive to learn, improve, and grow.

The act of giving is centered around helping others get better, and it is a very positive process. Those who give help others get better. They are naturally in The Giving Zone.

Throughout our lives, we will be presented with numerous obstacles, problems, and challenges. If we do not strive daily to learn and get better, we will use the same old solutions to solve new problems. This is a formula that guarantees continual failure.

Mary and George have a major disagreement in their marriage. When they want to do something for fun, Mary wants to get out, but George wants to stay home. Mary wants to go out for dinner, see a movie, or go on a hike. George wants to stay home, have a barbecue, rent a movie, or enjoy the sunset.

They have had many arguments about this issue for several years. Their conflict has become so deep that they have considered divorce. They both decide to get some personal training to help with their problem. Thus they expand their knowledge and skills in the area of relationships and communication.

They soon come up with new solutions. One solution is to do activities which encompass both their needs. George pretty much likes to stay put and not be active on their fun time together. Mary likes to be active and do something away from the home. So, they decided Mary could drive the two of them to a beautiful grassy area on a hill that has a great view of the sunset. He cooks the barbecue for the two of them. George can sit down, and enjoy the sunset and the barbecue. Mary is able to do something outside of the home. She enjoys being outdoors and takes a short hike.

If Mary and George hadn't been willing to get better (make changes), they wouldn't have solved their problem. Thus a major key to solving problems is self-improvement.

The willingness of people to solve a mutual problem is an act of giving. Each person involved has a willingness to help the other person in order to solve the problem. Each seeks new knowledge and discovers ways to improve the relationship. This attitude of mutual help, or mutual giving, is an essential ingredient needed to enter The Giving Zone.

Most important, if people decide not to get better in life, their problems will at best stay the same, but will more likely get worse. Many people wait for things to get better on their own. But things won't get better unless we get better.

Many marriages dissolve because one spouse wants to grow and get better and the other spouse doesn't want to make any changes. In this case, the one partner expands his or her horizons and will leave the other partner behind. They both have less and less to relate to each other about, causing a major disconnection problem. Both end up going their separate ways. Friends can experience a similar scenario.

How can a married couple prevent this problem? A very good solution is for the couple to set goals and plans for their marriage. The goals and plans contain their mutual interests. The spouses decide how they can expand their knowledge and participate in those interests.

Their planning can contain new areas of growth together as well as continuing what already serves them individually. Couples can take classes together and share in other ways to enjoy activities of mutual interest. It is also important for each spouse to have an individual life too. Each needs to have activities that are not done with the other. It is also very helpful for couples to revisit their goals and plans from time to time to reevaluate and improve upon them.

One spouse may have an interest that the other is willing to try to get involved with so they can share it together. This is a loving gesture.

My wife has had professional training in dance. Dance is very much her essence. I took ballroom dance lessons with her. It wasn't exactly my favorite thing and it was very difficult for me to learn at first. However, over a period of five years, I've developed a skill in ballroom dancing and enjoy it immensely. For my giving gesture of joining my wife in an activity that she loved, I have been rewarded with a love of dance that gives me extraordinary pleasure. In addition, dance increases our closeness, we meet interesting people, and we enjoy the excitement of entering dance competitions.

Businesses and organizations that are successful operate on a similar paradigm of always seeking improvement. Businesses and organizations that don't improve and keep up with the times will typically go out of business.

Public schools are a prime example of this. They either get better, or in certain parts of the country they could lose students and taxpayers' money. There are many private schools and home-schooling programs that offer a very good education. The public schools have to continue to improve or they may lose students, good teachers, and funding.

The real key to gaining knowledge is to set a high standard for achievement. It's about going for mastery. Most people only go for mediocrity at best. They do not study to master a subject. They do not practice needed skills to a level of mastery.

Mastery is defined as "possession of a consummate skill, the state or condition of having power or control, or full command of a subject of study." Mastery takes years. How long does it take a musician to attain the skill needed to play at Carnegie Hall? How long does it take an athlete to train to win an Olympic medal or to become a professional athlete? Typically, how many years does it take someone to learn leadership skills to run a very large organization? The answer is that it often takes 10, 15, or more years. Some goals may take a lifetime.

For example, in 1981 I decided that I wanted to master personal relationships. As of the time of this writing, it has been 24 years of working to master personal relationships. Have I achieved mastery yet? No. I believe that I've mastered only some parts of personal relationships.

In sharing more on ballroom dance, I've had hundreds of hours of ballroom dance lessons, most of them in the past five years. Have I achieved mastery yet? Not even close. Ballroom dance is so athletic that it recently almost became an Olympic sport. Compared to professional dancers who compete at that level, I'm very much a beginner. I take one or two lessons a week. The professional competitors may practice quite a few hours a day. However, as an amateur, I feel that I'm doing quite well. I love it. I have been consistently getting better by taking baby steps in the direction of mastery.

The key to having a great standard for attaining knowledge and results is to go for mastery. Mastery is an issue of integrity. *Integrity* means being whole. Mastery means going all out and getting the whole knowledge, thus being of integrity. Why do something half-way and lack integrity from getting only pieces of knowledge? Go for it all! Be the champion you are capable of being!

When you go for mastery in an area of your life, you are creating a masterpiece. Just as artists master each aspect of their art – mixing of paints, understanding color, brush work, drawing, oils, frames, etc. – to master any area of life, *you master each piece.* When you've mastered all the pieces, you have formed a *masterpiece.*

A golf professional, for example, needs to master many different areas of the game to create a masterpiece of success and winning. There is the mastery of the swing, which can take many years to perfect. There is the mastery of woods, irons, putting, greens, sand traps, and, very importantly, there is mastery of the mental part of the game. Many people who seem great in golf, freeze up mentally in competition. Their game falls apart.

How does Tiger Woods continually strive for increasing his mastery? After a game when the other players go into the clubhouse, what does Tiger do? He practices for hours. If his weakest area in the game was putting, he practices putting.

I encourage you to go for mastery in the attainment of knowledge, and the development of skills in your key life areas. It is not easy. At times it is arduous. At times it's also fun. It is worth it. Mastery is a major key to being able to contribute at a very high level, and it is a major key to success, prosperity, and happiness. It is one of the greatest sources of fulfillment.

In life, we are either getting better or we are getting worse in our key areas. We cannot just stay the same. If we do not improve, we will tend to get worse. This is because things are always in flux – they are changing. When you keep up with the positive changes, you can thrive.

Even one step better is to be able to stay *ahead* of the changes. We each have the ability to see some of the changes that are coming and to be proactive with them. Not only that, we can also be part of the forefront and create positive changes.

Knowledge is the key to expanding our horizons and improving our lives. Those people who continually gain new and important knowledge will be the leaders of our future. Those at the forefront of change actually create trends. Because they practice self-improvement consistently, continually expanding their knowledge, these masters of getting better become leaders who change society for the better too. Examples are Abraham Lincoln, Thomas Edison, Martin Luther King Jr., Bill Gates, Lee Ioacocca, Margaret Thatcher, and Oprah Winfrey.

One powerful tool we can use to get better on a daily basis is an affirmation by Emile Coue in a book written in the 1920's called *Autosuggestion*. This powerful affirmation is:

"Day by day, in every way, I am getting better and better."

This is a powerful affirmation we can repeat daily and implement in our lives.

A wonderful gift we can offer others and ourselves is to continually strive to get better. This will set you apart from others. You will be more filled with life, and all of life will increasingly become an adventure. You will become a great role model for others and make a vital contribution to the relationships you have with your family, your friends, and your work associates. Encourage others to get better, and you will be helping to make a better, more joyful world. You'll also bring more people with you into The Giving Zone.

CHAPTER 9 EXERCISE

The purpose of this exercise is to help locate areas in your life where it would be helpful for you to improve. Each area you improve in can help make other areas of life better too.

1. Is there an important area of your life that you are not improving much in – such as career, relationships, finances, health, etc.?

2. What ways could you improve in that area of your life? Make a list of these ways.

3. Take each way you could improve in and write what the consequences (results) would be of that particular improvement. List the consequences of each particular improvement until you have a realization of something important that gives you a deeper insight.

4. Repeat 1. to 3. until you've had a noticeable shift in awareness.

CHAPTER 10

ASKING QUESTIONS

"A prudent question is one-half of wisdom."
—Francis Bacon

*D*eveloping and utilizing the skill of asking questions makes you a great listener. In response to your questions, the other person talks in order to be heard. The more you allow the other person to talk, the more you will be appreciated.

Those who listen are actually considered to be great conversationalists. This is because nearly all people love to talk, to be listened to, and to be interviewed about their lives. It makes them feel important and there is a natural excitement about being discovered and understood. It creates a close connection between both people.

The key to asking great questions has to do with the strength of your ability to listen. If your ability to listen is highly developed, you will be very effective in choosing great questions to ask.

Listening puts you in the position of really showing that you are interested in the other person when you communicate. A person who is effective in asking questions is doing the opposite of the person who continually rambles on and on. The person asking questions is in a role of caring about others, whereas a person rambling on and on is showing disregard for others.

The following point is basic for having productive conversations in The Giving Zone: The person focused on asking the questions is in a giving mode, but the person who thinks it's all about talking as much as you can is in a taking mode.

Asking questions also gives you the ability to learn about the other person. You can ask questions based on what you want to find out about the other person. This is a very positive process that can result in the recipient feeling special and is a key to the process of developing friendships.

When you do this, you'll find out that asking questions is fun. An endeavor filled with creativity and discoveries, asking questions launches you on an exciting adventure where you'll truly get to know other people at a deeper level.

Again, this is a process of giving. Many people experience from time to time a feeling of loneliness. This is due to not connecting well with others. When you ask meaningful questions, it gets them to open up and creates an opportunity for bonding deeply. The strong connection developed is the epitome of giving and is a principal attribute of living in The Giving Zone.

The asking of questions also gives you control over the communication. You have the freedom to direct the communication largely where you want it to go. Without some control, the conversation can go in all directions and become meaningless and chaotic.

Most people feel like a victim when they communicate with someone who rambles on and on, engaging in meaningless conversation. The conversation continues in a negative fashion, and the one not allowed to talk is likely to feel upset. The asking of questions gives us the freedom to be able to direct the conversation towards a positive end.

Thus, there may be times that we may be listening to someone who talks nonstop, and we are totally frustrated by it. Rather than trying to break in to make a statement, a carefully selected question can direct the conversation toward a topic that is meaningful, and it can also benefit the other person involved.

Mary is talking with Bill at a lunch break. Bill has been rambling on incessantly. She and others in the office have experienced him many times talking for 20 minutes or longer without stopping. Unfortunately, the topics he chooses are of little interest to others.

Mary, not wanting to have to experience Bill's incessant habit one more time asks him a question to direct his interest outside of himself. After Bill tells about something he likes and pauses for a moment, she asks, "Bill, you know what I'd like? I'd like it if you were to ask me about the dance contest I competed in last weekend."

Bill complies with Mary's wishes and asks her about the dance contest. Bill is thus engaged in finding out about Mary. Mary feels fulfilled from the conversation.

There is an exception to the problem of dealing with an incessant talker. Some people genuinely have no one who cares enough to listen to them and really need someone who will listen. In this case, if you will just take the time to fully listen and take interest in what is said, it can be extremely helpful and even healing to that person. It may take an hour or two to listen to all that person needs to say, but it is well worth it.

The key is just to listen and not to judge them.

Another advantage to using questions is that we can direct people away from destructive communication.

Steve is starting to pass gossip to Robert about a co-worker. The gossip is malicious and filled with lies that are designed to destroy the co-worker's reputation.

Robert does not want to be a participant in the gossip. He immediately cuts Steve off at the pass by asking, "What is your purpose in telling me this?" Steve says, "Um, Um, I thought you might want to know this, but I guess not." Steve immediately changes the topic back to his favorite subject – golf.

Taking the gift of asking questions a giant step further, one can develop an effective sequence of questions that will steer the conversation toward a constructive outcome.

Remember, a *process* by definition is "a series of actions, changes or functions that bring about an end or result." Thus, one can design a series of questions to help bring about a particular end or result. According to Alan Walter, a planned sequence of questions can also be thought of as a *process*.

For example, champion salespeople have a sequence of questions planned out to help the prospective customer arrive at the decision to buy. Leaders may also plan a sequence of questions in order to inspire their followers to go in a beneficial direction. Consultants, coaches, and trainers can use a correct sequence of questions to help their clients attain their wants, goals, and dreams.

Those who efficiently and consistently use effective sequences of questions to help bring about beneficial results for everyone involved are the masters of communication.

To learn such a skill is invaluable. Ask questions and inspire others to ask questions. Study and train to increase your ability to ask specific questions, and to ask them in the right order. You will be sharing a skill that will open the doors of communication and the hearts of many who will experience the joys of living in The Giving Zone.

CHAPTER 10 EXERCISE

1. Make a list of people you would like to get to know at a greater depth.

2. Pick one person from the list and write some questions you could ask to get to know that person better.

3. What outcomes are likely to happen by asking these questions to get to know this person better? List possible outcomes until you've had a realization of something important that gives you deeper insight.

4. Repeat 2. to 3. over and over until you experience a significant shift in your awareness.

CHAPTER 11

DEVELOPING CHARACTER

"Maturity is achieved when a person postpones
immediate pleasures for long-term values."
—Joshua Liebman

T his chapter on character development is closely related to the chapter on the gift of honesty. This is because the quality of honesty is an extraordinarily important character trait.

Character may be defined as "moral or ethical strength; integrity; fortitude." People of strong character are rare. They practice persistence and courage. They do not give up. When they take up a cause or a mission, they will typically stick with it until they triumph. They also tend to have the ability to motivate others into developing the character to achieve their purposes and goals. Being of strong character is a quality of people who give extensively and a requirement for living consistently in The Giving Zone.

People who develop great character have a presence that is healing to the people around them. Character gives us a collection of tools that we can use as directors of our lives to create Academy award–winning life performances.

A person of character is continually giving the gift of virtue. The expression of virtue transforms the lives of many. When you are around a person of great character, you are likely to feel a sense of excitement and purpose. A person of character can motivate others to achieve their dreams and aspirations.

Such people have developed many virtues such as honesty, integrity, persistence, love, compassion, enthusiasm, purpose, the ability to connect, charity, vision, organizational skills, sincerity, the ability to save and invest a portion of their earnings, humility, and the ability to listen.

A favorite quote of mine is from Napoleon Hill, from his book, *Law of Success*. It is the most powerful quote regarding character that I've come across thus far:

> *Character is the philosopher's lodestone through which all who have it may turn the base metals of their life into pure gold. Without character, you have nothing; you are nothing; and you can be nothingæ. Character is something that you cannot beg, steal or buy. You can get it only by building it; and you can build it by your own thoughts and deeds and in no other way.*

Those who are devoid of character lead destructive lives. Without character, one leads a life without much regard for others. Those who are rich in character lead a life that adds value and that is of great benefit to others.

Character is acquired through the development of virtues. Many of the great teachers on the planet have stressed the development of virtues. These great teachers were major participants in The Giving Zone because they devoted their life to service and made the world a much better place for us to live in.

Each virtue is a "gold mine" that contributes to an individual's success, power, and happiness. A virtue is a building block upon which each of us can forward our purposes and goals while also helping others to achieve their purposes and goals. Without developing virtues, an individual will experience a failed life, poverty, and misery.

Benjamin Franklin in his autobiography shares a system for developing virtues. He selected a list of 13 virtues to work on. These virtues included enthusiasm, order, resolution, sincerity, justice, cleanliness, tranquility, humility, and industry.

Each week he would take one virtue and focus on it daily for that week. After 13 weeks, he would start over and work on each virtue for the next 13 weeks. After a year, he had worked on each virtue four times.

Frank Bettger in his book, *How I Raised Myself From Failure to Success In Selling*, discusses Benjamin Franklin's system and suggests that you take each virtue and write up a brief summary on a 3 x 5 card. You carry the card around with you throughout the day so that you can work on reinforcing it.

When I utilized Benjamin Franklin's system I experienced a significant increase in my ability to give to others, as well as increased personal success and happiness. I have also used other effective systems to develop virtues, which have helped build character.

When I lived in Hawaii during the eighties, two of my teachers, Loy and Robert Young, had their students keep a checklist and check off the virtues that they were working on. They also suggested that people contemplate on a particular virtue each morning and plan how to implement it in their life that day. This was very helpful in holding us accountable to developing that virtue.

The building of character is paramount to cultivating the ability to communicate with and influence others. Napoleon Hill in *Law of Success* describes what happens when people compromise their conscience and their personal beliefs:

No man can afford to express, through words or acts, that which is not in harmony with his own belief, and if he does so, he must pay by the loss of his ability to influence others.... If you compromise with your own conscience, it will not be long before you will have no conscience; for your conscience will fail to guide you, just as an alarm clock will fail to awaken you if you do not heed it.... and it is only when I speak from a heart that is bursting with belief in my message, that I can move my audience to accept that message.

Alan Walter has discovered a very powerful key to the development of character. He writes in his paper "Get Closer to God" that the infinite attributes of God – such as love, honesty, knowledge, power, justice, and leadership – are all within us. The following quote from the Bible (Genesis 1:27) reads:

"So God created man in his own image."

God is the exemplary role model. Since it's in our nature to express God's image, it's important for us to take responsibility to duplicate the qualities that God has in order to come closer to God. Mr. Walter states, "As one duplicates God's attributes, one finds that the Spiritual Power within oneself begins to flow forth."

A person who possesses great character is the quintessential example for others to follow, showing that virtues can be in alignment with a higher purpose. Thus the person with exceptional character leads the way and has a positive effect on the lives of many. This valued person is part of the vanguard in The Giving Zone.

CHAPTER 11 EXERCISES

The purpose of these exercises is to strengthen your character traits. This will result in an increased ability to give as well as increase your success, prosperity, and happiness.

EXERCISE ONE

1. Make a list of character traits in which you tend to be strong.

2. Select one of the character traits and write down the consequences (results) you and those connected to you have because of this character trait of yours. Keep writing these consequences until you have a realization of something that gives you a deeper insight.

3. Repeat 2. over and over until you've had a significant shift in awareness.

EXERCISE TWO

1. Make a list of character traits that you find are lacking in yourself.

2. Select one of the character traits and write down the consequences (results) you and those connected to you have because of your lack of this character trait. Keep writing these consequences until you have a realization of something that gives you a deeper insight.

3. How could you strengthen that character trait? Think of at least two ways.

4. Repeat 2. and 3. over and over until you've had a significant shift in awareness.

CHAPTER 12

USING CONSTRUCTIVE CRITICISM

*"There is a principle which is a bar against all information;
which is proof against all argument; and which cannot fail to
keep a man in everlasting ignorance.
This principle is contempt prior to examination."*
—Napoleon Hill

It is a gift to be able to criticize others constructively. Constructive criticism is helpful; destructive criticism is harmful, and one of the most negative processes there is.

Critical means: "characterized by careful and exact evaluation and judgment."

The destructive criticizer has an ulterior motive such as taking revenge, releasing temper, expressing jealousy, or tearing down other people to make them fail. There is no "careful and exact evaluation and judgment."

Constructive criticism has the intent of helping others.

The motive here is indeed to carefully and exactly evaluate and judge. The attitude is also one of genuine concern and respect for the other person. To live our lives without exact evaluation and judgment puts us in chaos and destruction. Effective parenting, for example, is a continual effort in evaluation and judgment regarding children. And, effective management means continuous evaluation and judgment of staff in order to gauge their performance.

Those who do not hesitate to give positive criticism to others are a great asset. They are courageous individuals who offer us the great gift of helping us grow and improve. They are true citizens of The Giving Zone.

On the other hand, how does it feel to hear destructive criticism? Have you known people whose primary communication style is to destructively criticize the people in their lives? Often these people will say, "I'm telling you this for your own good."

I find this type of statement highly questionable because the harshly critical person is usually not so noble. People who express criticism harshly usually do it for their own gain. Perhaps their motivation may be to vent their feelings, to convince you they are right, to make you think they are superior, or to control you.

Do you ever find yourself being destructively critical of some of the people around you? I used to have this flaw in my communication style years ago. I often criticized others harshly.

Recognizing the destructiveness of this style of communication, I embarked on a journey of seeking consulting and training to overcome this pattern. The changes I made transformed my life – it has made all the difference in the world between having positive and enjoyable relationships versus negative and painful ones.

So many times we are destructively critical of others when we actually want to help them. We feel that they will do better next time because of what we say. However, the opposite is likely to occur. The people we so negatively criticize are most likely to be offended, and they may rebel, withdrawal from us, or even be weakened further.

Destructive criticism is one of the worst forms of abuse. Its effects can be devastating.

One of the things I've dedicated my life to is positive communication tools developed to help end this type of abuse on the planet.

I personally have used positive communication tools taught to me by Alan Walter, and I have also taught others to use these tools effectively. When we learn to let go of a negative communication style, it results in major positive changes for ourselves and for many of the people with whom we come in contact.

First, it's important to note that criticism is an important part of the communication process. When it is done constructively, it can be very helpful – and even a gift. When it is done destructively, it can backfire and accomplish the opposite of what you wanted.

Destructive criticism ruins marriages and businesses, and contributes to illnesses. It discourages people and can cause people to give up on their dreams and goals. It closes the stage productions in life before they have a chance to open.

Sometimes people think that they need to be critical of someone, yet it is uncalled for. In many instances, the people being criticized just want to be heard and appreciated.

The person who already tends to be overly critical will make it a habit of criticizing others in any situation possible.

You share some positive news with a friend, but your friend says something negative such as, "You should have done better." You are surprised by your friend's response because you just wanted to be appreciated and heard. Instead, your friend is trying to find something wrong with what you are doing to help you improve. But all you feel is disheartened and misunderstood.

Another problem that can occur with negative criticism is that people giving the criticism believe they are only being truthful, but they are actually being revengeful. The real motive behind the harsh criticism is revenge.

> *June feels very uncomfortable about the criticism she gets from her husband. One evening he tells her that he's finally going to tell her the truth. He raises his voice, and in an angry, vengeful tone, proceeds to dump a lot of complaints on her.*
>
> **He wasn't interested in communicating the truth. He used the truth as a façade to communicate revenge. And behind the revenge was the purpose of blaming her for all of his problems.**

Constructive criticism, by contrast, is a communication tool indispensable to success. It has its place in the business world, in school, in the sports world, in the family, and in any area of life that could use improvement.

With the attitude of constructive criticism, you are there to help the people with whom you are communicating. A major distinction in constructive criticism is the communication of what is being done well in addition to what can be improved. The destructive criticizer will only look for and communicate what is being done wrong.

It's important to always give a suggestion for improvement whenever you offer constructive criticism.

> *John tells his employee that he is doing it all wrong. John promptly walks away. The employee is confused and doesn't know what to do because there was no suggestion for improvement.*

If you are not sure if the criticism you are getting is constructive, check to see if the person gave you a suggestion for improvement. If a suggestion of improvement wasn't offered, the criticism was not constructive, and the motive of the criticizer was likely to be destructive.

Another abusive trait of destructive criticizers is a perfectionistic attitude. They have contempt for anything not perfect. Remember what we discovered earlier:

"Perfectionism is the ultimate sabotage."

Most people will procrastinate or quit if they have to be perfect. Perfectionism doesn't allow people to make mistakes – which is a vital part of the formula for success. The perfectionist says:

"You've got to get it perfect or you are no good."

The perfectionist breaks hearts and destroys dreams. Another problem about negative criticism is that it often creates opposition and rebellion. The people being criticized are so offended that they fight back by being uncooperative.

Jackie is a schoolteacher who is extremely critical of her students who misbehave. Several of her students fight back by intensifying their misbehavior. They refuse to do their schoolwork, they cut class, and a couple of them cheat on their tests.

Robert is harshly critical of his 17-year-old son who "has a bad attitude." His son is surly, refuses to do chores, and eats in front of the TV instead of coming to the dinner table. The more Robert criticizes his son, the more disrespectful and rebellious he becomes. The problem comes to a head when Robert's son is caught vandalizing property.

Many people who are in such a state of rebellion will *want* to fail at what they are doing in order to win. The student who is in total opposition to the hypercritical teacher will fail in order to defeat his teacher. In failing, he wins.

A similar scenario frequently occurs at work. An employee has deep animosity for the overly critical boss who keeps telling him what a terrible job he is doing. The boss has such a negative view that he now expects that his employee will fail. The employee is so upset that he sabotages himself by doing the poor work the boss expects in order to get even and defeat the boss by making him look bad. The employee wins by losing.

An important skill to develop is the ability to encourage others by using positive criticism. This is the gift many great leaders possess. The people receiving the criticism may not always like what they are hearing, yet they still feel respected.

It's evaluation time for Spencer. He's a bit nervous, but he's actually looking forward to it because his employer, a sales manager, shows a lot of thoughtfulness and appreciation during the evaluation process. When his employer tells him that an area of improvement needed is to increase his number of sales calls, Spencer doesn't feel hurt.

This is because his sales manager says it in such a way that Spencer knows he cares. Also the employer communicates a lot of appreciation for what Spencer does do well on the job. Spencer walks away feeling encouraged and so strongly cared about that he is doubly committed to doing a great job and will be determined to help his employer succeed in the process.

To be free from giving destructive criticism and instead only giving constructive criticism – this is an essential skill to offer the world. To make this shift is a valuable journey in which we leave the darkness for the light. It is a worthwhile, life-changing process that will heal individuals, families, organizations, nations, and even the world. It places us firmly in The Giving Zone

CHAPTER 12 EXERCISE

The purpose of this exercise is to develop the ability to be constructive in your criticism. This involves not only suggesting what needs to be improved, but also includes encouragement.

1. Name someone to whom you would like to give positive criticism (family member, friend, associate, etc.).

2. What is the positive criticism you would like to give?

3. How could you word it to be most effective?

4. Write down a number of consequences (results) that could come out of this constructive criticism. Write down these consequences until you've had a realization of something that gives you a deeper insight.

5. Repeat 1. to 4. until you've had a significant shift in your awareness.

CHAPTER 13

USING THE
MIND AS A FILTER

*"When we create a thought it is telepathically projected
into the universe at a certain rate of vibration.
Thoughts are also magnetic and attract energy of the same
vibration. This is the universal Law of Attraction.
Choose your thoughts well; like attracts like."*
—Alan C. Walter

*U*sing the mind as a filter is like giving a vital gift to yourself because the thoughts we allow into our mind largely dictate the success and happiness we attain and help others to attain. It is also an essential key to being in The Giving Zone, where positive thoughts thrive. You won't be able to give for very long, or be of value to others, when you maintain negative thoughts.

Each of us has the power within us to choose negative or positive thoughts. A negative thought focused on long enough will develop negative fruits. A positive thought focused on long enough will develop positive fruits.

Napoleon Hill says:

...the human mind responds, in kind, to whatever thought impressions it receives.

This means that the thoughts we allow ourselves to receive create effects in our lives. There are two basic ways we receive thoughts. The first is from a source that is external to ourselves. This includes input from other people, the environment, and the media. The second source of thoughts is from within ourselves.

The conscious mind is the part of the mind that is aware or conscious of what we are thinking. The subconscious mind is the part of the mind that is unconsciously thinking. It works continually, even in our sleep. A strong part of our reality is created from the subconscious mind.

The key is to regulate the thoughts and ideas that come into our minds instead of just letting anything come in.

If, for example, a person lets continual negativity to enter the mind, the subconscious will tend to focus on the negative and that person will typically create a life of negativity. On the other hand, people who allow positive thoughts and ideas to continually enter the mind will tend to create more positive results in their lives.

I have done a number of things to regulate the thoughts and ideas that come into my mind. For example, I decided to greatly reduce the amount of violent TV programs and violent movies I watch. I also decided to surround myself with people who have a positive attitude in life. I read positive books such as autobiographies of famous people and books that help me grow personally, and I listen to my mentors on audio tapes at home and in my car. In addition, I frequently take self-improvement seminars from people I consider to be some of the top mentors in the world.

In this way, I have quite a bit of control over what

*comes into my mind. By cultivating more and more posi-
tive thinking, particularly centered around my life purpose,
I am able to have a more contributing, productive, and
happier life.*

It is not a quick or easy task to learn to be in charge of the
thoughts and ideas that we allow into our minds. It typically takes
a commitment of many years, a commitment that offers great
rewards for people who seek to achieve discipline in their thinking.
These people who can focus their thoughts in the directions they
want, have true power and the ability to contribute at a high level.

In 1875, Mary Baker Eddy wrote in *Science and Health*:

*We are all sculptors, working at various forms, molding and chis-
eling thought.*

**Albert Einstein told us back in the 1920's that everything
(including our bodies) is composed of energy.**

Alan Walter writes:

Every thought is composed of energy.

Thus, each one of us needs to decide what kind of energy we
want – positive and constructive, or negative and destructive.
Positive thoughts composed of positive energy will tend to create
positive results, and negative thoughts composed of negative energy
will tend to create negative results.

**The other side of this coin is that we can run into a problem
if we feel we need to completely restrain what we think and feel.
We can become frustrated if we believe we cannot have any negative thoughts or negative feelings whatsoever.** *What matters is how
we handle those thoughts and feelings when they come in.*

All beings are dichotomous in nature. Dichotomous here refers to two contradictory parts. Examples are night and day, hot and cold, hate and love, positive and negative. Each of us normally has positive thoughts and emotions as well as negative thoughts and emotions.

A most important skill to develop is to learn how to deal with negative thoughts and emotions.

One main thing is not just to hold them in. Research has shown that people who continually stuff their anger can manifest a number of physical illnesses such as ulcers.

How can we best handle our troubled thoughts and emotions? There are a number of ways we can begin this process. Since we are continually dealing with thoughts and feelings, the optimal way to handle them is to decide to study and master the whole arena of thoughts and feelings. This can be started through reading books, listening to tapes, and, best of all, through individual and group mentoring.

There is a lot to learn. For example, each "negative" emotion in and of itself may not be bad. What is important is to be in charge of each thought or emotion, and to use it for helpful purposes. An example of this can happen while attending a funeral. We will experience the prevailing mood of grief. The key is to match the mood, and thus communicate in the mood of grief with the family members who had the loss. Then we can connect with them so that they feel loved and supported. This way of communicating will transform negative energy into positive energy.

Another example is that there are times when it is appropriate to express anger. In a team sport at half time when a team is losing, the coach may express in different ways, "Come on, we can do it." The coach expresses this in anger to motivate the team, which can have an inspiring effect – and even help the team win.

Anger can also be helpful in those situations where people are angry at themselves for not performing well at something. If I lose a tennis match I can turn my game around after getting angry with myself, telling myself, "I can do better than that."

We spend our lives continually handling thoughts and emotions. Even in our sleep we do this. It is well worth the investment to gain more knowledge and understanding in this area.

Another way to help dissipate troubled thoughts and feelings is to share them with another person. It is important that this person can understand and relate to what you're going through. It can be a close friend, a consultant, or a spiritual leader. This person needs to be someone with experience in listening fully. This confidante also should be someone who is trustworthy to keep all that is said confidential. Such a special helper needs to be able to express understanding and compassion for our thoughts and feelings. The listening, understanding, and compassion make for a healing experience.

There are many situations when we can benefit by sharing our troubled thoughts and feelings rather than keeping them bottled up.

For example, I won over an audience composed of members of an organization called Catholic Charities. I said, "I have a confession; I'm a bit nervous." The audience laughed and fell in love with me. An audience can feel a little uncomfortable when they come to see a speaker they haven't heard before. To share a human emotion can create instant rapport and trust.

There are seminar programs that teach people how to work with their thoughts and emotions. Since I'm in the field of personal betterment, I've been attending many such seminars over the years, and I've also been teaching and coaching others in this special area.

People who make great strides in the area of regulating their thoughts and emotions have the potential to succeed at a very high level and to give great value to many others in the process. It is pivotal for creating outstanding stage productions in life. This is a special and rare skill to develop and apply towards the achievement of one's dreams and aspirations, and a way to set up permanent residence in The Giving Zone.

CHAPTER 13 EXERCISE

You can improve your ability to catch your negative thoughts and turn them to positive thoughts through this exercise. After doing this practice exercise a few times it's recommended that you practice it in your life during each day as much as possible, where you can also practice catching negative thoughts and turning them into positive thoughts.

1. Write down a negative thought you have about something. (Example: I don't have enough money.)

2. Write down a positive thought you could have about that thing. (Example: I'm working toward having more money.)

3. Repeat 1. and 2. over and over until you have a good shift in awareness.

CHAPTER 14

BEING TRUTHFUL RATHER THAN HAVING TO BE RIGHT

"Life is lived at many levels. Lived in false levels,
you will be in miseries, pains, and poverties. Lived in the true
level, you will experience joys, pleasures, and richnesses."
—Alan C. Walter

One of the most pervasive conflicts we tend to experience in life is the "I'm right, you're wrong" battle. One has a point of view, the person who is arguing back has another point of view, and both try to prove that the other person is wrong.

The "I'm right, you're wrong" battle destroys marriages, businesses, societies, and nations. This is because the person claiming to be right is more concerned with being right than with being truthful. Their communication is likely to contain lies. Any nontruth is a negative process that instantly takes people in the direction of failure.

Remember, when we are not truthful we will move in a destructive direction. When we're truthful we will move in a constructive direction. The ability to let go of having to be right, and choosing instead to be truthful, is strongly connected to the process of giving, and thus will move us into The Giving Zone.

If it's more important for us to be right than truthful, our communication contains non-truths and we're taking from others. When it's more important to be truthful to others, we're giving to them.

We offer a precious gift when we can let go of the "I'm right, you're wrong" game and replace it with simply being truthful.

The problem with saying, "I'm right, you're wrong" is that it very seldom works.

People don't like to be told that you are right and they are wrong. How do we feel when someone argues with us in a routine everyday matter? For example, a person arguing with me says, "You're wrong for thinking the toothpaste tube should be rolled up. I'm right; it should just be squeezed." My impulse is to defend my position, because it's a put-down to be told I am wrong.

The tendency for anyone in such a scenario is that we feel put down and we want to regain a position of strength. So we reply, "I'm right, you're wrong."

The basic problem with the "I'm right, you're wrong" argument is that "right" often differs from the actual truth of the situation. In a conflict between people, truth and rightness are often different.

Here's a vivid example. Two cars arrive at a four-way stop sign. The driver on the right got to the intersection first. Thus he has the right-of-way. The driver on the left ignores the law that he is supposed to yield to the driver on the right. He proceeds through the intersection first.

The driver on the right is furious about the driver on the left not yielding the right-of-way. The driver on the right, "being right," pushes hard on the gas pedal to get through the intersection first. An accident results with serious injuries.

The driver on the right was certainly "right" about having the right-of-way and was "right" about being able to be the first one across the intersection. However, he caused serious injuries in his rightness. Here's an important question to ask: Was he truthful in his action?

A definition of *truth* is "conformity to knowledge, fact, actuality, or logic." It also means "sincerity, honesty, and integrity." The driver on the right was "right," but he was not truthful. In fact, he was nearly "dead wrong."

Another example is an argument between a husband and a wife. The wife is upset that her husband is leaving his clothes around the house without putting them away. Also he won't even pick up his dinner plate to put it in the dishwasher. He feels "right" about not contributing around the house because the family he grew up with picked up after him.

The orientation of his family was that women do the work around the house, so he believes it's not a man's job. She was raised in a family in which everybody helped around the house, both male and female; there was a sense of equality.

They both work full-time and both are tired when they come home. They are both "right" with their point of view. In the culture he was raised in, men didn't do housework. In the culture she was raised in, there was equality between the sexes.

They have heated arguments over this issue for years, continually yelling at each other, "I'm right, you're wrong." Finally on the threshold of divorce, they take a class in How to Have Optimal Relations and discover the truth of their situation, which differs from who is "right" and who is "wrong."

She understands that in his macho culture, it was forbidden for men to help around the house. He understands that she was raised with a belief in equality. He also admits that she is just as tired as he is when she gets home from work.

They begin to discuss solutions wherein he can choose tasks to do around the house that he feels are more masculine. He chooses to throw out the garbage, polish the furniture, and sweep and vacuum the floors. She is patient not to rush the transition to more equality. She realizes how strong his cultural programming is. He also understands that his wife works full-time and needs help with housework.

Making someone wrong is a form of abuse.

When I say I'm right and you're wrong, I'm automatically setting up a conflict because I take no responsibility for my actions. I'm using blame and solving the problem with an accusation.

My underlying message is, "everything is your fault." "I have no responsibility in the matter." "I'm doing nothing that needs to be improved." "You need to change, not me."

When we put the problem on the other person and take no responsibility for ourselves, we put the other person in a corner – and that person is likely to fight back.

Rightness and truth are often two entirely different things. People will often use rightness to win their argument with little or no regard for the truth.

When you catch yourself and another in an "I'm right, you're wrong" battle, stop the game. If you don't know what else to do, take a time-out.

One way to break the cycle is to admit the truth of what you yourself are doing to contribute to the problem. The other parties will then be encouraged to reciprocate and share their responsibility in the matter. Again, this is The Law of Reciprocation at work.

A father has an argument with his arrogant son. His son (Bob) is critical of his mother who is computer-illiterate and has difficulty doing simple things on the computer.

What ensues is a "right-wrong" game. Bob says, "Mom is really being dumb." Father says, "You're wrong. You have no right to talk about your mother that way." Bob says back to his father, "You're wrong, my five-year-old brother knows a lot more about computers than Mom."

Fortunately, the father takes a relationship skill workshop and learns tools to break the "right-wrong" cycle. One evening he goes up to his son Bob and says, "Your mom needs help on the computer. Would you please help her?" Bob agrees to help.

The father has made a big change. Instead of having to be right about his son's negative behavior, he simply drops his negative attitude and asks for help. The son, perceiving a change of attitude, has nothing to fight against and helps his mother.

The following instance clearly illustrates what happens when "I'm right, you're wrong" is replaced with truth.

Susan has a disagreement with her husband Pete over how to raise their children. She feels that she is right and her husband is wrong. Susan feels that her husband is too strict. Pete feels that Susan coddles the children and lets them "get away with murder."

The more they fight the "I'm right, you're wrong" battle, the more polarized they become. Pete becomes more strict and stern and Susan coddles and spoils the children even more.

Finally, Susan decides to get out of the battle altogether by recognizing a moment of truth. She realizes that both she and her husband have valid points. She sees that if they will listen to each other and find what would truly be helpful to the children, they will work out some form of agreement. They set up a time for discussing the problem. Susan, having more clarity on the subject, starts off by asking her husband to say what concerns him about their child-raising methods.

He immediately goes into how she coddles and spoils the children. This time Susan really listens for the truth of the situation and admits that there are indeed instances of her coddling the children too much.

She asks him for help in working with the children to become more resourceful and responsible. After a couple more such meetings, Pete actually softens and begins to be less strict.

Truth will win out in such situations because it is far different from the "I'm right, you're wrong" battle.

To sum up, when you play the "I'm right, you're wrong" battle, you are not interested in truth. You are interested in winning and defeating the other person involved.

Truth sidesteps this game by getting to the actuality of what is happening. The people involved have to take responsibility for each of their roles in the problem. With an uncovered truth, all sides tend to listen, cooperate, and come up with a solution in which everyone can win.

We offer a powerful gift when we let go of the "I'm right, you're wrong" game. It gives us the ability to work through conflicts by being truthful – an important attribute for living in The Giving Zone. In being truthful we take responsibility for our own actions and then we can be helpful to the other people involved as well.

CHAPTER 14 EXERCISE

You can become more aware of your "I'm right, you're wrong" thoughts by doing this exercise. Get out of the right/wrong game by looking for the truth of the situation.

1. Is there someone in your life with whom you play the "I'm right, you're wrong" game?

2. Name a way you play the "I'm right, you're wrong" game with this person.

3. What are the consequences (results) of having to be right? Write down the consequences until you've had an important insight.

4. What is the truth of each situation that would have you being truthful rather than insisting on being right?

5. Repeat 2. to 4. over and over until you've had a realization of something that gives you a deeper understanding.

6. Repeat 1. to 5. over and over until you have had a shift in awareness.

CHAPTER 15

BEING ACCOUNTABLE INSTEAD OF USING BLAME

*"And since you know you cannot see yourself, so well
as by reflection, I, your glass, will modestly discover
to yourself, that of yourself which you yet know not of."*
—William Shakespeare

There is an addiction from which nearly all human beings suffer. It destroys marriages, it destroys businesses, it destroys lives, and it destroys nations. People who overcome this addiction reach one of the highest achievements and contribute immensely to those they touch. They have a very giving posture in life and are active participants in The Giving Zone.

I've been working on overcoming this addiction since 1978, when I became aware of it. It is one of the most pervasive addictions of all. As of the writing of this book, I have not completely overcome this addiction, although I've improved immensely. It is the addiction of blame.

"She did it to me."

"It's his fault."

"If it weren't for you, I would have succeeded."

"You've ruined my life."

Blame is not only acted out in words; it is also embedded in thought. And our thoughts are very instrumental in creating our reality. Thought precedes verbal expression. Verbal expression precedes action. Action precedes results.

What does it feel like to be around someone who blames you or other people? Have you ever noticed when someone blames you, that person is inferring that the problem that you are *both* having is completely *your* fault? And furthermore, the person is in essence telling you that it has always been your fault, and that it will always be your fault.

What is worse, people who blame you in this way will also try to convince you that they are perfect and have never done anything themselves to contribute to the problem.

When these people are having their "blame fix," they will try to make you feel like you are the devil and they are an angel.

It can be very helpful to look at the times you have blamed others. Namely, when you are blaming another person, you will tend to try to place all fault on the other person. You will try to persuade the person you're blaming that the problem you're both having has nothing to do with you.

One of the most powerful quotes that I've ever come across from Alan Walter is:

"All blame is a lie."

The reason blame is a lie is because when we blame, we take no responsibility for how we may have contributed to the situation. Blame is projected onto the other person, making it completely the other person's fault.

As a consultant for 33 years, I've observed many marriage and business problems in which each party is blaming the other.

A husband may say, "My wife doesn't take care of the house, she is critical of me, and she avoids me." He takes no responsibility for what he does to contribute to the problems of the marriage. His argument consists of blaming her for everything that is wrong with the marriage. He infers that he is perfect and she is the only one at fault.

When you hear what the wife has to say, it's entirely the husband's fault. She says that he comes home from work, he turns on the TV, he has a few beers, and he won't talk with her.

An employer blames his employees for the problems at work. He says they show up late and do only just enough to get by. The employees blame the employer. They say that he doesn't care and that he pushes them too hard.

If blame is a lie, what does communication look like when it's blame-free? The answer to this question is simple. Honest communication involves both sides taking responsibility for what they themselves do to contribute to the problems involved. Each individual holds themselves accountable for their part of the problem.

A husband might say, "My wife and I are having some problems. I know that I'm contributing to our problems because I turn on the TV when I get home and refuse to talk with her even though she wants to be able to talk with me." The wife might say, "I contribute to our problems by not doing the things around the house I promise and by being overly critical."

An employer might say, "I cause problems with my employees by being too pushy and not listening to their concerns." An employee might say, "I don't show much initiative on the job and I need to get to work on time."

This is the superior type of communication that is very giving in nature, and helps us gain entry into The Giving Zone.

How do we break the blame addiction? A first step is to understand an important principle. When we blame or complain about others, we are blaming them for the same or similar thing that we have actually done in our own lives.

An example is the husband who complains that his wife avoids him. He says she won't be intimate with him. It turns out that he has been avoiding her. When he comes home from work, he hides from her by watching TV and drinking beer.

Another instance is the employer who complains that his employees are not on time. He has major tax problems because he is two years late on paying taxes. Here is one of the areas in his life where he himself is not on time.

In relationships, business or personal, we are often mirrors for each other. What we complain about in another is actually something about ourselves that we really don't like. Napoleon Hill says in *Law of Success*:

Like attracts like! There's no denying this! Literally speaking, every person with whom you come in contact is a mental looking-glass in which you may see a perfect reflection of your own mental attitude.

When you blame someone you are in a relationship with, you may not have done the *exact* same thing that you are complaining about, but it is very possible that you have done something similar even if it's remotely similar.

An example is a wife who complains that her husband is an alcoholic and gets drunk every day. It turns out that he drinks a half a bottle of whiskey per day and is indeed an alcoholic.
She has not had a drinking problem at any point in her life. She doesn't even drink and never has. However, she has an addiction that is similar. She is very overweight from

grossly over-eating. She will go from the donut shop to the pizza shop and get intoxicated on food. From eating too much food, she goes into a drunken stupor and neglects key responsibilities in her life.

Another example of people doing something similar to what they blame another for is the employer who complains that his employee steals money from the cash register. The employer truly has never stolen money. However, he cheats on his taxes and is thus also stealing money in a different way.

When we blame the person we are in a relationship with, there is a major problem which occurs that becomes detrimental to the blamer. We give up our power to that individual. When I blame someone, for example, if I say, "It's because of her that my life is no good," I am saying that she is in charge of me and I can't do anything about it. She has to stop doing what she is doing for me to get better. She has the power. I'm helpless. I'm a victim.

The price we pay for the habit of blaming is we turn off our power switch and hand it over to the person we blame. This is a formula for losing and failure. This is the "victim game" many people play in their relationships. It is sad that such victims choose to cast themselves in heartbreaking losing roles in their stage productions in life.

Overcoming the blame addiction takes some doing. However, it is one of the greatest investments we can put our time and energies into constructively.

My life is at least 1000 percent improved due to my work on letting go of a blame addiction.

Some steps in overcoming blame are:

1. Find out what you are doing that is the same or similar thing to what you are complaining about. This will help you be less upset about the other person because you will see that you are complaining about something you yourself also do.

2. Communicate from a place of accountability in solving the problem with the other person. As a first step in communication, share what you are doing that contributes to the problem. The Law of Reciprocation will tend to work with you at this point. The person will become more likely to admit responsibility too. However, in some instances, the person you are having a problem with may resist admitting to having any responsibility for the problem. Often people who blame others for their problems are so upset that they will not look inside themselves to get to the truth of the situation. It may take time before they are willing to take responsibility for their actions.

3. Take classes that teach relationship and communication skills. This can be of great value in moving toward overcoming blame. I've not only taught such classes, but I have also taken quite a number of such classes over the years as well. Working toward letting go of the habit of blaming, and replacing it with the habit of taking responsibility for our actions, is an invaluable asset to offer – to ourselves and to everyone with whom we come in contact. It is one of the most powerful positive processes we can use. Taking responsibility for our actions is a magnificent act of giving, and it is a vital trait of those who are active participants in The Giving Zone.

CHAPTER 15 EXERCISE

This exercise is designed to help move people from blame to responsibility.

1. Is there someone you are in a relationship with whom you blame for a problem you are both involved in together?

2. What is the problem you blame this person for?

3. Is there some way you may have contributed to that problem? Look for even a small way you may have contributed to the problem.

4. What are the consequences (results) of the way you contribute to the problem? List the consequences until you've had a realization of something that gives you a deeper insight.

Sample answers:
1) Husband.
2) He is very argumentative with me.
3) I disagree with him a lot and actually rarely listen to him.
4) He gets more upset with me when I keep disagreeing with him. He rarely feels that I'm on his side.
   It keeps us distant from each other.
   It makes the children upset.

5. Repeat 1. to 4. over and over until you experience a shift in awareness.

CHAPTER 16

HAVING A DEFINITE AIM INSTEAD OF A COUNTER AIM

"You and I are essentially infinite choice-makers.
In every moment of our existence, we are in that field of all
possibilities where we have access to an infinity of choices."
—Deepak Chopra

*I*n this chapter we will talk abut the ability to achieve the aims and goals that are truly what we want, rather than counter aims that give us the opposite of what we want.

When we have an aim or desire to achieve a goal, if we do not achieve that goal, but instead achieve the opposite of that goal or something else, it could be that we actually hold a counter aim or counter goal. This counter aim or counter goal is also known as a "hidden agenda."

To clarify: When we have a counter aim it means we have a hidden agenda or unconscious plan to achieve a result that we really don't want.

It needs to be stressed that this operates at an unconscious level. We set a particular objective and work toward it – perhaps for years – yet we do not reach that goal. We achieve something else that we didn't want. As directors of our stage productions it is as if we start out with an idea of a happy comedy type of production and instead we end up with a tragedy. If we follow a hidden agenda, we end up with a production of life that is very different from what we truly want.

Have you set a goal, yet achieved something far different?

Perhaps we want to increase our income for the year; yet, at the end of the year we have made less money and piled on more debt. Perhaps we do increase our income, yet we increase our debt also, so we are worse off.

Or we want to lose weight; yet we end up gaining weight.

If we have an aim to achieve one thing, yet in fact we achieve the opposite, again it could be that unwittingly we are holding onto a counter aim or a hidden agenda to make sure we actually achieve something we don't want.

A great example is a client I had who could not increase her income no matter what she did. As a consultant I knew that she had a counter aim to make sure that she would always be broke – even though in her heart of hearts she wanted to have more money.

It turned out that years ago she was told that if she kept her income below $20,000 per year, her daughter would be eligible for a college scholarship. At that time she unconsciously made the decision to earn very little. Years later she had forgotten this unconscious aim. She just saw that no matter what she did, she was always broke.

The key here is to understand that unconsciously she had made an earlier decision to dramatically cut back her income.

Another client of mine was on the verge of his second bankruptcy. I could see that he had a counter aim or hidden agenda to be broke. Sure enough, he had a hidden plan to make sure he stayed broke. When he was a child, his father kept telling him that money was evil and that wealthy people were evil. His father believed that wealthy people got their money from using people, from lying, and from stealing.

My client loved his father very much and unconsciously eagerly modeled some of his father's negative beliefs, including the belief that money was evil. When my client started to make a lot of money, unconsciously he became very uncomfortable because of this hidden idea that money is evil.

Unknowingly, when money started coming in, he felt he was evil and had to get rid of it. He was simply following what his father had told him. Thus, he was unconsciously working hard to have very little money (to not be evil).

I've been married for 18 years. However, many years ago I had a difficult time finding and staying in a personal relationship. I actually had a hidden agenda to make sure I wouldn't find someone to relate to closely.

The hidden agenda was that I had equated giving up freedom to being in a close relationship. I thought that being in a close relationship meant I had to give up my autonomy.

With this belief, I unconsciously worked hard to stay out of relationships, to make sure I would be free. Of course the belief was false, but I based my reality on it until I *learned to let go of it. Then I found my mate.*

This example relates to one's ability to operate in The Giving Zone. If we set a goal of contributing to another, and yet we have a counter aim or hidden agenda, it is likely that we will not be able to give to that person after all. Undiscovered hidden agendas can keep us locked out of The Giving Zone.

Why would someone have a counter aim or hidden agenda? One principal cause of a counter aim or hidden agenda has to do with self-worth. Each individual feels a certain amount of self-worth. If your self-worth is low, your financial worth will tend to be low. Your relationship worth may also be low, resulting in painful and difficult relationships.

If your self-worth is high, you will tend to have optimal finances and much better relationships, and you will likely also be more effective in other areas of your life.

Susan really wants to have a great relationship with a man. However, she continually gets into relationships with men who are verbally abusive and give hardly any love. It turns out that Susan holds a counter aim, which is to get very little from men because her self-worth is very low. She feels she is not worthy of love, and worse, she is unconsciously working hard to punish herself.

Alan Walter says:

"We are doing what we are doing when we are doing it."

This means if we are losing in an area of life, we are doing what it takes to lose and we are operating on a hidden agenda to make sure we lose. If we are winning in an area of life, we are doing what it takes to win and we are operating with a positive aim or positive agenda to win.

It is essential to point out here that there are scenarios that may appear as if a counter aim or hidden agenda exists, but it isn't so. For example, when you set a brand new goal, and you are not winning at it immediately, it probably does not mean that you are operating on a hidden agenda. If you decide to become a professional musician, for example, yet you have no experience playing an instrument, you know that it typically takes quite a few years to develop the music skills to achieve your goal. Thus, if in six months, you're not getting booking engagements, it probably doesn't mean that there is a hidden agenda.

There is a learning curve to every skill we want to develop. Keep an eye on what you are seeking to achieve. It is very possible that I may have a hidden agenda if I have been working on an objective for a long time, and I *do* possess the skills needed, and yet I still haven't accomplished my goal.

Most people blame others or circumstances for their struggles and failures in life. The key is to understand that we are largely responsible for the results we get in our life. If we are willing to really look and see what we are doing to land at the results we are getting, we can greatly improve and have a much better life.

This includes the area of counter aims and hidden agendas. We are responsible for any counter aim or hidden agenda we have. It's our responsibility to make the decision to seek the wisdom that will allow us to discover and discard these negative programs.
It is a great gift to be able to work through our counter aims or hidden agendas to be able to achieve our dreams and aspirations. It is a grand and rare gift to be able to liberate others effectively from their hidden agendas.

To locate and work through our hidden agendas is not easy because they are indeed hidden and unknown. It is likely to take a skilled and trained individual to help us spot and work through them. Some training companies are designed to help people free up their hidden agendas in order to attain their dreams and aspirations. I have been developing this skill many years, both in my personal goals and also in the training and coaching of others. It has been extraordinarily helpful to develop my awareness in this area.

When you see someone who is continually losing over an extended period of time, it is very possible that the individual has an unconscious plan to lose. To be able to communicate the concept of counter aims and hidden agendas to such a person is a great skill. To have the training to help people work through it is an even greater skill. It is a journey worth taking to uncover the truth. The greater the truth, the greater our success, our freedom, and our happiness, and the better the contribution we will make in The Giving Zone.

CHAPTER 16 EXERCISE

The purpose of this exercise is to help you spot hidden agendas that may be blocking you or others from achieving goals and purposes.

1. Do you have a goal that you have been working on for a very long time that you are not succeeding in? (Examples: You stay in debt instead of getting ahead financially. You have not been increasing the number of sales in your job. You don't seem to be able to get in a close personal relationship.)

2. Do you have a possible hidden agenda to make sure you don't achieve your goal? (Examples: You don't feel you deserve to be wealthy. You dislike your job. You don't want to get close in a relationship because you might get rejected.)

3. What are possible solutions to eliminating this hidden agenda? See if you can come up with at least two possible solutions.

4. Repeat 1. to 3. over and over until you experience a shift in awareness.

CHAPTER 17

LOVING TO GIVE RATHER THAN PLAYING THE MARTYR

"Choose a job you love, and you will never have to work a day in your life."
—Confucius

This topic is at the core of what The Giving Zone is all about. It is the love of giving. The difference between loving to give and not wanting to give is as great as the difference between day and night. When we love to give, we experience pleasure and naturally move into The Giving Zone. When we dislike giving we experience pain.

The more you love to give, the greater are the benefits for the others involved and for yourself. The more you don't like to give, the fewer the benefits for the others involved and for yourself.

This is a favorite chapter of mine because it's about a primary reason I wrote this book. I mentioned before that I had a big transformation – from being somewhat resistant to giving to loving to give. This had the effect of a vastly improved life. Because I love to give now, and I give so much more, in return I receive so much more – help, support, friendship, love, opportunity, etc. It has moved me farther into The Giving Zone.

A major cause of not liking to give comes from the experience of giving everything you've got, and getting nothing back in return. The person who experiences this may feel like a martyr.

It is parents who give everything to their children, wait on them hand and foot, and the children who do not give anything back. They won't do their chores or their schoolwork and they even resent their parents.

It is the spouse who gives freely to the other and feels like it's all for nothing, only going in one direction.

It is the employee who works long hours, feels underpaid and gets no appreciation.

It is the employer who works very hard to give employees nearly everything they ask for, pays them well, and gets only complaints in return.

The word martyr in this context is defined as "someone who endures great suffering and makes a great show of suffering in order to arouse sympathy."

The martyr will tend to experience suffering from giving tremendously and getting little back. And, in numerous ways, the martyr tries to elicit sympathy for this suffering. Martyrs may try to give the appearance of being a good person because of their suffering. However, the martyr is not playing a good or helpful role, whether in personal relationships or in business relationships. The martyr is actually filled with resentment and hatred, expressed either overtly or covertly. This is a very negative process.

There is a lot of destruction involved in playing the martyr role. A number of serious problems result from it:

1. When you suffer as a martyr, it tends to cause the people around you also to suffer. This suffering is destructive to relationships.

One key aim martyrs have is to make other people feel guilty for how bad off they are. It's through a demonstration of suffering and resentment that martyrs try to make other people feel guilty.

"Look what you did to me."

"You're wrecking my life."

"I'm working myself to the bone."

The problem is that when you try to convince other people how bad they are, they will tend either to fight you back, withdrawal from you, or experience lowered self-esteem. Any of these consequences is destructive.

2.   When you play the martyr role, you tend to want sympathy from others. In order to get it, you need to make sure that you are suffering. In order to suffer, it means that you need to show people how bad off you are because of what they are doing to you.

To be bad off means that your aims and goals are set unconsciously toward the direction of making sure that you will lose and do poorly.

Thus to be a martyr is to be invested in losing.

To try to arouse sympathy, the martyr will unconsciously lose in order to get that sympathy. This unconscious investment in being bad off and losing will cause poverty, loss of relationships, and numerous potential health problems.

It's interesting that people rarely do actually give the martyr sympathy. This is because they are typically reeling from the emotional pain caused by the martyr, or because they are smart enough to avoid participation in the martyr's game.

It is typically not helpful to give the martyr sympathy. To give the martyr sympathy just adds fuel to the martyr's game of suffering, being a victim, and making others feel guilty.

3. As a martyr you will tend to be depleted of energy, because suffering and resentment drain one's energy. In addition, you will probably lower the energy of those around you.

The resentment of the martyr and the hatred that results is a very fatiguing experience. This lowered energy can affect other areas of one's life. When a person is a martyr, or is often around a martyr, their personal relationships may suffer, their work may suffer, and their leisure time may suffer.

What is the solution to this problem?

How can we overcome the martyr problem and the dispensing of resentment? How can we give freely and unreservedly in our relationships without feeling like we will be taken advantage of?

We can begin to handle this problem by learning to give intelligently and by looking at three types of giving:

1) **Giving from resentment or martyrdom**
2) **Giving on automatic**
3) **Giving freely from the heart**

I have shared what happens when we give while playing the martyr role. The results of that type of giving tend to be destructive to all involved, including the martyr.

Giving on automatic is the second form of giving. This is the type of giving we can get locked into from too much repetition, from too much routine with no new learning or change involved.

One example is the factory worker who has the task of doing one simple task over and over thousands of times a day. A second example is the postal worker who only sorts mail all day long. The teacher who has been teaching the same lessons for many years to mostly disinterested students is a third example.

The third type of giving comes from the heart. The person gives freely, loves to give, and even acquires new knowledge in the process.

To give freely does not mean that you give blindly. You give intelligently. To give intelligently you educate people to give back. You also choose the recipients.

In a later chapter we will discuss intelligent giving more in depth.

There is a law that is similar to the Law of Reciprocation, called the Law of Equitable Exchange, which, when followed, enhances the process of giving for everyone involved. This law means that in order for the process of giving to be effective, we ought to require an equitable exchange. When we give equitably, we can give freely. This usually involves having an agreement about what you will get back in return. These agreements are set up in both personal and business relationships.

It is worth noting that this law applies somewhat differently when we're talking about charities. You may give freely and not expect anything back. However, exchange is still involved in the process.

You may give to a charity because you appreciate the abundance you have in life and you want to give something back. Also when you give to a charity, you may want those who receive your gift to have an opportunity to give something back to others. This encourages self-sufficiency rather than dependency. (See the upcoming chapter on giving to charitable organizations for more information.)

Through the understanding of giving intelligently and equitably, you can give freely to your children, because you are teaching them to contribute back – through household chores, earnestly doing their schoolwork, or with a simple thank-you, etc.

If we do not educate our children to give, they will be spoiled. To spoil children is to forget to teach them generosity – and spoiling weakens them. The capacity to give is one of the most important abilities that exists, and it's vital that we instill this quality in our children early in life.

A child who is spoiled will have a much lesser chance for success in life. Spoiled children typically get out in the world and expect everyone to give to them, just as their parents did. The consequence is that these children aren't very motivated to work hard or to contribute to the lives of others – essential aspects to being successful.

The same thing applies to all people to whom we give. We need to encourage the recipients to give back. Whether in the work world or the world of family and friendships, intelligent giving always involves encouraging others to give back.

At the same time we give freely, we want to educate and encourage others to give freely. We do not want to have a monopoly in the area of giving. *If I am the only one giving, I am actually being selfish.* I need to allow others the same privilege of giving.

In some situations it's good to demand that others give back.

Again, let's look at the example of families in which the parents continually give to their children, and their children won't give anything back. In this situation parents may need to demand that their children give back.

If employees are continually late and are doing poor-quality work, it is appropriate for the employer to demand that they improve their work or risk being fired.

When you teach and encourage others to give, you are also giving them a great gift.

Many people do not have any conscious awareness that something is wrong in the level of exchange in their relationships. Some of us think that we just need to give, and that people we give to will already know how to give back to us.

Communication is the key. You've got to tell the recipients what you want or it is very possible they won't know.

Some people think that teaching others to give back to you is selfish. The truth is just the opposite. We actually do harm to those in our personal and business relationships if we give and do not receive back from them. They know deep down inside that they owe us and have an obligation. They have a debt to pay us that festers inside them. They typically feel guilty until they can give something back in exchange.

Have you ever given quite a bit, and the person on the receiving end didn't give back to you, yet resented you? The reason for this is that such people know deep down inside that they owe you something.

There is a sense of obligation and a sense of guilt. Rather than facing up to that obligation, they throw their feelings back on you by resenting and blaming you.

This is why so many spoiled children resent their parents.

I had an experience years ago in which I realized how much my parents had given to me – their time, their effort, their sacrifice, and their love. At that moment I realized what a debt I owed to my parents. I had tremendous gratitude for what they had given me and I wanted to give back to them as fully as I could.

Sometimes it may be appropriate to ask the person who is receiving from us to give back to someone else, as proposed in the book *Pay It Forward* by Catherine Ryan Hyde. This is especially true in volunteer and charity work, but it can also apply in special situations in our business or personal life.

Cassandra takes on a special project by helping her sister get a job. It has involved helping her write a resume and coaching her on interviews. It has taken a lot of time and was done with great love. Her help made all the difference in the world in getting the job she wanted.

Cassandra doesn't want anything back from her sister, yet requests that her sister do the same thing for someone else. Cassandra and her sister are very happy about the exchange. Her sister is looking forward to finding someone she can help. From the knowledge gained in getting the job, she has lots to offer others in their career search.

There are no hard and fast rules concerning the exchange involved in giving and receiving. It is a creative process, and fun when you learn to give intelligently.

Those who master the art of intelligent giving have much to offer the people in their lives. When a group of people learn to give intelligently they can create an endless cycle of people giving to people. This is the great flow of reciprocation that can affect millions of people. This giving cycle results in better families, work places, societies, and nations – and makes for a better world.

One more note on this subject pertains to the highest form of giving freely from the heart. It is the type of giving that is aligned with what Napoleon Hill calls our Definite Chief Aim. This comes from the belief that each of us has a unique life purpose. This Definite Chief Aim is the mission each of us has in life.

One of the most rewarding things to experience is watching people give who are involved deeply and passionately in their Definite Chief Aim or life purpose. These people may become masters of their craft.

As shared earlier, I have experienced powerful transformation in my life by greatly increasing my giving. For instance, I may be at a conference, and I suggest an idea to someone that proves to be helpful. On an airplane I may help someone in the seat next to me solve a problem. Sometimes I console a family member.

New friendships form more quickly, tremendous appreciation is expressed to me, and my business opportunities expand. Then there are more people being of help to me, more people I can help, and so on. And life is more fun!

Whatever you do, give freely. Do the best job you can to give to others and encourage them to give freely too. Your rewards will be spectacular. The Bible says in Galatians 6:7:

Whatsoever a man soweth, that shall he also reap.

Napoleon Hill shares:

The Divine Economy is automatic and very simple: "We receive only that which we give."

Give wholeheartedly. You will build a big bank account to receive many riches and you will hold a master key to the door to The Giving Zone. You may not get a return on your investment at the moment. You may have to wait months or even years. However, you will indeed get a good return on your investment eventually, and at the same time you'll be a gift for the many people you touch. It is a great law that operates for us all without fail when we participate in it. It makes us very successful directors of the winning stage performances in life.

For those who want to explore intelligent giving at a greater depth, I recommend that you study the issue and receive training in the area. Look for mentors to help guide you. This can greatly accelerate your awareness and your abilities to fully give and receive.

CHAPTER 17 EXERCISE

We all have the choice to be able to give joyfully rather than to give as a martyr. This is an exercise to learn to change from being a martyr in giving to giving from joy.

1. Do you have a situation in your life in which you feel like you are giving as a martyr?

2. What is that situation?

3. What are the consequences (results) of giving like a martyr in that situation? Write down these consequences until you've had a realization of something that gives you a deeper insight.

4. How could you solve this problem so that you could give from joy instead of as a martyr? Think of at least two different solutions.

5. Repeat 1. to 4. over and over until you've had a shift in awareness.

CHAPTER 18

LIVING YOUR
LIFE PURPOSE OR DREAM

*"There are many things in life that will catch your eye,
but only a few will catch your heart. Pursue these."*
—Michael Nolan

If we want to really make a difference, each of us needs to be
living our life purpose. Our life purpose is of a spiritual nature
because it is concerned with the essence of who we are and what
we are here to contribute. This is a subject at the heart of The
Giving Zone and what it takes to be more fully a part of it.

Those who are living their life purpose become a major inspiration, igniting the dreams and aspirations of many others. They
are the Academy award–winning star actors on the stage of life.

Napoleon Hill writes: "It is most appalling to know that ninety-five percent of the people of the world are drifting aimlessly through
life, without the slightest conception of the work for which they
are best fitted, and with no conception whatsoever of even the
need of such a thing as a definite objective toward which to strive."

Remember, Alan Walter says:

Your dream is the conduit to your power.

Several changes take place when we conceive of our main dream in life. We suddenly have a tremendous amount of attention and focus. And then we possess a new vision of a bright future.
Walter continues:

It is these bursts of Dreams and Aspirations that give certain beings the power and strength to conquer their environment and adversaries and go on to produce great events and achievements.

If you don't feel in touch with your life purpose or a major dream about which you are passionate, there are a number of things you can do.

First, make a list of what you are truly passionate about – things you really love to do. It could be something you like to do for fun. It could be a hobby. On your list, there is quite possibly something in the direction of your life purpose and you can develop it into an income.

It is important to know that your life purpose stems from the essence of who you are. There is immense enthusiasm and passion involved once it's identified and made a reality. This is because our individual essence contains tremendous enthusiasm. The original meaning of *enthusiasm* is derived from the Greek meaning "inspiration in God." There's a reason the Bible says we're made in God's image and likeness. This also explains why those who love their work enjoy it so much that there is little difference between work and play.

James A. Michener writes:

The master in the art of living makes little distinction between his work and his play, his labor and his leisure, his mind and his body, his information and his recreation, his love and his religion.

He hardly knows which is which. He simply pursues his vision of excellence at whatever he does, leaving others to decide whether he is working or playing. To him he's doing both.

Going back to your list, pick one activity that you are passionate about. Ask yourself the following two questions: 1) How can I earn money from this activity? 2) How can I turn this into a career? Next, ask yourself the specific steps you can take to bring this activity into actuality, and write down your answers. Now you can follow that plan.

Second, make sure that what you choose to do from your list contributes positively to other people and the planet. The greater your contribution, the closer you are likely to be to your life purpose.

Third, it is very important to cultivate a burning desire to find your life purpose. Stay open. If you truly want to get in touch with your life purpose, and you focus on it, you will be led to it. In time, you will meet the appropriate people, come across a book, a teacher, mentor, or a speaker, and you could be on your way to becoming unstoppable in the accomplishment of your dream. The Giving Zone is the playground for those who are living their dreams.

If you work on seeking, finding, and expressing your life purpose for a long time and still feel no closer to it, it's likely that you have an inner obstacle blocking you. You may have a hidden agenda (see Chapter 16). Also, in this case you'll find that locating the appropriate mentor or trainer may help you on your way.

Each of us has a spiritual essence within us that radiates our life purpose. It is the "real you" within each of us, containing a unique code for our contribution to the world. It is paramount for an authentic life. It is either restrained or activated. Seek it, find it, and once it's realized, free it, activate it, emanate it, and stay the course.

CHAPTER 18 EXERCISE

If you want help identifying or clarifying your life purpose, reread this Chapter and take the three steps recommended.

CHAPTER 19

GIVING ABUNDANTLY

"I don't think you ever stop giving. I really don't.
I think it's an ongoing process. And it's not just about being
able to write a check. It's being able to touch somebody's life."
—Oprah Winfrey

The ability to give freely with virtually no restraint is a gift of stellar importance. The rewards for people who truly operate at this level are unlimited. The doors of The Giving Zone are wide open.

When we learn to give as little as possible and try to get as much as we can, this is a sure formula for failure. Though people may profit in the short run, they will most definitely fail in the long run.

The Law of Reciprocation is at work 24 hours per day, seven days per week. The less you give, the less you get back. The more you give, the more you get back. It works this way perpetually for everyone. Some people call this karma.

Highly successful people are highly contributing beings. Doesn't it make sense that success is the result of the amount of your contribution given to the world?

Thus, those who contribute the most are going to be the most successful.

Napoleon Hill in his book, *Law of Success,* has a chapter entitled, "Give More Than Paid For." He writes that in every job he had, he gave more than he was paid for. The effect of this work ethic was that in a number of job situations, he started from the bottom and worked his way to the top because he always contributed so heavily.

He would stay beyond normal working hours and find out from his boss how he could be of further help. He would not get paid for the extra work at the time. However, the promotions he got and eventual success cultivated from his attitude more than amply paid for his abundant giving. Using this principle he even became one of the owners of a company.

Most people would rather do the opposite.

"I'm not going to do it if I don't get paid."

These people do not know that they are proponents of a formula for losing in life. They are the first to be let go in a tight job market. In recent times, there has been an increase in downsizing, layoffs, and firings. The people who give more have a much better chance of staying employed; and if they are let go, they'll have a much better opportunity for getting another job. Business owners who give more are following the same recipe for success. They will go the extra mile for their customers as well as their employees.

My wife is a great model for giving abundantly. She continually asks the people she knows and meets, "How can I help you?"

A friend of ours was nominated for a major art award and there was to be television coverage. My wife wanted to know how she could help this friend. We ended up flying to the event directly so we could be there to help our friend for a few days in any way we could. The help we gave her made a big difference in how the event went for her. She got the help and support she needed and it was a lot less stressful. In the meantime, we learned a great deal from the experience and made connections with people that were of benefit to the advancement of our own work.

Giving freely is a big part of the formula for making friends. By definition, a friend is an ally. An ally is someone who partners with you.

You partner with others by giving and helping. This is also the formula for prosperity and setting up residence in The Giving Zone.

When you have friends, family, or associates visit you, do you want them to be taking as much from you as they can? Or would you prefer they contribute, help make things easier and more fun? The answer is obvious for most of us. We enjoy being around people who are contributors.

As employees on the job we need to take responsibility for the whole company, including our superiors. The head of a company listens every day to people asking for raises and asking for other kinds of help. What do you think would happen if you were to come into the office and let the boss know that you want to do anything you can do to help? This is a major key to how you'll succeed in your career. Expressing this can-do attitude will make you stand out from the rest.

Think of all the ways you can help others in your life. Make a list. Go to these people and offer your help.

This does not mean that you should become a martyr and be taken advantage of. There are people who may have a propensity to take and give nothing back. There is nothing wrong with asking these people to give something back in exchange for your hard work.

Bob Trask, a seminar leader and trainer, teaches the concept of allowing others to give "to you." This may seem like the opposite of what is being taught in this book. However, there are actually many people who tend not to give. When we allow these people to give to us and teach them how to give to others, they can also learn to be givers, and the cycle will continue.

Abundant giving is a key formula for success and happiness.

When a group of people is abundantly giving and receiving something of value, all the individuals involved are increasing the prosperity of others as well as of themselves. And if they are united toward a key purpose, their results will be magical – in helping many individuals make their dreams come true. All people can then play their unique role in The Giving Zone.

CHAPTER 19 EXERCISE

This exercise is designed to help you give more abundantly.

1. Choose an individual, group, organization, etc. that you would like to give to abundantly.

2. Describe how you can give abundantly in this situation.

3. What would be the consequences (results) of your giving abundantly in this situation? Keep writing the consequences until you've had a realization of something that gives you deeper insight.

4. Repeat 1. to 3. over and over until you've had a noticeable shift in your awareness.

CHAPTER 20

GIVING INTELLIGENTLY

*"It's not that I'm so smart, it's just that I stay
with problems longer."*
—Albert Einstein

To give freely means to be able to give without having to get anything back. This type of giving can create miraculous results for the giver as well as for the people who are the recipients of the giving.

It makes for an ever-expanding group of people living happily in The Giving Zone.

However, if we constantly ponder about what we'll get back, this puts the brakes on any chance at genuine generosity. Giving wholeheartedly, without expecting anything in return is what I call "intelligent giving." However, there are some parameters for giving wholeheartedly:

1. Do you give some thought and planning about the recipient to whom you are going to give?

You probably would not want to give to the criminals who prey upon people. However, in certain circumstances you many want to help people who have had a criminal past.

> *One such example is a friend of mine who gives unrestrainedly to people who have a criminal past. He is a trainer who works with the prison population. He gets very good results in helping prisoners to change their thinking to a positive and constructive mindset. With this new mindset, they are more likely to have a more constructive life while they are still in prison and also when they get out in the world again.*

You may also want to give freely to those who value what you have to offer. It can be upsetting to give your time to someone who does not really value what you offer. On the other hand, giving to someone who truly values and appreciates your skill and attention can be a total pleasure.

2. Is what you are giving beneficial in nature to the recipient?

For example, is what you are giving going to empower the recipients, or make them dependent on you? If it makes them dependent on you, you will end up weakening them.

> *Steve is concerned that he is not really helping his friend Larry when he does Larry's job for him at work. Steve is a very able negotiator in his job at a law firm. Larry is new on the job and is having some anxiety about using his unproven negotiation skills.*
> *Steve offers to help Larry by doing some negotiations for him. Steve is very skilled. Larry just sits back and lets Larry do the whole negotiation time after time.*
> *After awhile, Steve realizes that he is not really being of*

help to Larry, but is accomplishing the opposite. Larry is becoming dependent on Steve. Each time he does the negotiation for Larry, Larry becomes more and more unsure about his ability to negotiate.

Finally, Steve suggests that he will do part of the negotiations and Larry will do the other part. Over time Steve will do more and more of the negotiation until he is doing the whole negotiation on his own.

Now Steve is truly helping Larry by teaching him to become self-sufficient. Eventually Larry becomes one of the top negotiators of the law firm.

3. Is what you are giving something you want to give to others?

If people repeatedly ask you to do things for them that you dislike doing, you are going to end up unhappy about giving those things. You might feel like a martyr about it and not only feel unhappy, but make the other person feel unhappy because of your misery. In addition, the quality of your giving is likely to suffer if you do not like what you are doing.

4. Is what you are giving wanted by others?

If we are giving something to people that they don't want it could be a waste of time. For example, we might give of our time to do favors for people thinking we are doing it for their own good. Yet, it is something they never wanted. Or we may feel that we have an obligation to give something to certain people, but what we are giving them is not what they want.

5. Does what you are giving allow the other person to give something back in exchange?

Remember, it weakens people to take and not have an opportunity to give back. You are giving a gift when you teach people to give back. They can either give back to you or to someone else.

There is nothing wrong with encouraging the recipients of your giving to give back.

The question may come up – How about giving to charity? Don't we give to charitable organizations without any thought of return? Not necessarily. There are some charities, such as Habitat for Humanity, which encourage or even require the recipient of the benefits to participate and give something back.

When we help people to become self-sufficient, our giving becomes much more effective.

My wife and I were at an outdoor market. There was an artist who had a very special product that we knew would help lots of people. We started sharing with her some ideas to assist her in getting her product marketed in a big way. She found our ideas very helpful. A couple of days later she called us and we gave her further consultation that lasted a good part of an hour.

She found these additional ideas to be immensely helpful. She then asked if she could give something to us in exchange for our time. We said we would love to have a piece of her artwork. She was very happy about the suggestion. We empowered her by allowing her to give back something of value.

Sally has been giving her time freely to her friend Tom. She has been helping him with difficult math problems for a college course. It has taken up quite a few hours of her time over a period of weeks. It turns out that Sally now has a need that Tom could help her with. Tom is very skilled mechanically and could help repair some things around her house. She asks Tom for his help: "In exchange for all the tutoring in math I've done for you, would you please help me fix a few things around my house?" And Tom is more than happy to give something back.

People often feel a sense of obligation, debt, and guilt if we so generously give to them and don't ask them to give back in some way. This key ability to prompt others to give back is a foremost ability for living happily in The Giving Zone.

What can we do if the person we are giving to refuses to give something back? We can ask why that person does not want to give back. If discussing this concern does not resolve it, it may be better to decrease or stop how much we give that person until that person is willing and able to contribute too.

Giving to others wholeheartedly is one of the ultimate gifts we can offer and one of the most positive processes there is. When we follow these important parameters we can empower our giving to create the greatest good for all concerned.

CHAPTER 20 EXERCISE

This exercise is designed to help you increase your ability to give intelligently.

1. Is there someone in your life with whom you feel that the giving is out of balance – you give quite freely, but this person gives back very little to you?

2. How can you give more intelligently – what can you do to balance the giving so that you receive more equitably?

3. What would be the consequences (results) of both of you giving intelligently (both giving and receiving equitably)? Keep writing consequences until you have a realization of something that gives you a deeper insight.

4. Repeat 1. to 3. over and over until you have had a genuine shift in your awareness.

CHAPTER 21

MAKING OTHER PEOPLE INDEPENDENT

"Discipline is the soul of the army. It makes small numbers formidable, procures success to the weak, and esteem to all."
—George Washington

*H*elping others to be independent is a gift that will restore families, marriages, friendships, and businesses. A lack of independence can be very destructive to relationships. Many people are in relationships in which one person is overly dependent on another. Dependency is the result of too much giving. The dependent person takes and takes, and gives little or nothing back. This is a formula for always staying locked outside of The Giving Zone, and is a basic cause of poor performances on the stage of life.

The person who fosters the dependency often is resentful and feels drained of energy. The person who fosters independence will typically be energized by it and can take part in The Giving Zone.

Remember, our experience is dualistic in nature. The opposites we know – cold/hot, night/day, darkness/night, good/evil, love/hate, poverty/wealth, fear/courage, pain/pleasure, etc. – teach us that our life is set up with opposite forces. Even our physical bodies have opposing forces. There is pressure from the atmosphere exerted on our body and there is pressure from the inside of our body exerted outside. These two opposing pressures are equal and keep the body in its present form. If they were not equal, the body would not keep its form and would not be able to survive.

Those who have the ability to handle the major dualities of life are rare beings who are an asset to us all. Not only will they tend to have a higher quality of life, but they can help many people have a vastly improved existence as well.

One important pair of opposites where balance must be maintained is between dependence and independence. Again, a problem can occur if one gives too much to another. To keep from fostering dependency in others, it is helpful here to define three stages of giving.

1. When we give too much, it can cause dependency.

This can occur when parents give too much to children and spoil them. It can also occur in friendships or in work situations when one person does all of the giving.

2. You give freely to others while encouraging them to give freely back.

In this stage, you're aware of the consequences of making someone dependent on you. Therefore, you decide to inspire that person to give back to you.

> *Jackie has a friend Gail who continually calls her and asks for advice. Gail always takes from Jackie and rarely offers to give anything back. Gail becomes dependent on Jackie and the relationship is very one-sided. Jackie does all the giving and Gail does all the taking. Jackie is concerned. She feels drained because Gail will not even ask to find out if there is anything she can do to help Jackie in return.*

One evening Gail once again calls Jackie for advice. Jackie is in a down mood from a problem in her family. Jackie doesn't even bring it up and Gail doesn't ask if she can help. At the end of the conversation, Jackie feels exhausted. Gail doesn't feel much better, because she saw that Jackie hadn't been her usual cheerful self.

This problem only continues to get worse – until Jackie discovers this second type of giving. Jackie decides to give Gail a call.

She says, "Gail, you may have noticed that sometimes when we have been together lately, I haven't been my usual chipper self. I wanted to let you know that I've been upset because of a problem in my family. My eldest son's teacher keeps calling me to let me know that he is doing very little of his schoolwork. I realize that I need to spend some special one-on-one time with him. I rarely have any time to talk with him or show interest in him. But when we do have special time for just the two of us, he seems to improve in school and at home. I was wondering if you would be willing to help me out. Would you be willing to watch my two other children one evening, so I'll be freed up to have some special time with my son? I figure you must appreciate all the time I give you. Wouldn't it be great for you to be able to give something back to me?"

By doing this, Jackie is teaching Gail to give back. Now their relationship can begin to be less one-sided.

3. In the third type of giving, all those involved give freely.

There is a magic flow in this form of giving. It involves people who can be independent as well as cooperative – a rare quality. The key ingredient that makes this type of giving work well is communication. All those involved communicate openly about their needs and wants.

Another characteristic of people who participate in this type of giving is that they tend to be very much themselves. They are not easily manipulated. They can ask for what they want, and at the same time offer to help others to get what they want.

Autonomous and cooperative people have the ability to be interdependent. This means that they can be independent, yet also be cooperative and work as a team.

The ability to help other people achieve independence is a very powerful and rare skill. So many people find themselves in situations where they feel that they are doing all of the giving and getting nothing back. They become bitter and weary of playing the martyr. To help others become strong in the area of giving sets them up to win and have a much more positive life. In the process we win, too, and then each of us can play our own unique part in The Giving Zone.

CHAPTER 21 EXERCISE

The purpose of this exercise is to learn to help other people become more independent.

1. Is there anyone in your life who is inappropriately dependent on you? If so, how is this person dependent on you?

2. Think of at least two ways to help this person become more independent. What would be the consequences (results) of having this relationship free of this dependence? Write down consequences until you have a realization of something that gives you a deeper insight.

3. Repeat 1. to 2. until you've had a noticeable shift in your awareness.

CHAPTER 22

RECIPROCATING EFFECTIVELY

*"No man, who continues to add something to the material,
intellectual and moral well-being of the place in which he lives,
is left long without proper reward."*
—Booker T. Washington

*T*he gift of reciprocation involves a basic principle governing all human interaction. Some form of reciprocation is involved in all human interaction. It can be positive or negative. Positive reciprocation means that there is give and take – a form of exchange is taking place. Negative reciprocation means only one-way giving is taking place.

The Giving Zone is a realm of positive exchanges between the participants who enjoy the fruits of both giving and receiving. They participate in a perpetual giving-and-receiving cycle that emanates outward like ripples on a lake affecting the many people who are touched.

To follow the principle of reciprocation, we can still give freely, but we need to study the consequences of our giving to be sure everyone will benefit to the maximum.

As I've mentioned, it's always important to ask yourself what the consequences will be when you give.

Rick volunteers for a charitable organization where he gives his time to high-risk young people who are unemployed and need financial help and guidance. The goal is for them to be able to get a job and keep it, allowing them to be self-sufficient.

Rick spends quite a bit of time over a period of a month working intensively with a 22-year-old man named Eric, who ends up getting a fairly good job through Rick's help. In looking over the history of this young man, Rick sees that he has had quite a few other people help him also. Eric has received help more recently from job programs, and earlier from boys' clubs.

Rick shares with Eric that he has given lots of valuable help to him and that many others have also provided help. Rick then encourages Eric to give something back in gratitude. Since Eric has been helped, Rick suggests that he could give the same type of help to others who have been in a similar predicament.

Eric appreciates what has been done for him and thus he agrees to give something back. Rick is very happy to help facilitate this, so he helps Eric get involved in The Big Brothers' Program. This is a program in which a child who needs guidance and mentoring is assigned an adult volunteer who can be like a big brother to him.

A week later, Eric has gotten together with his new 11-year-old pal named Roger. He and Roger toss a football, and Eric gets to know Roger and starts to help him so that he won't make the same mistakes he made, and hopefully he'll have an easier time growing up and some day starting a successful career of his own.

Of course there are emergency situations such as natural disasters when people are in desperate need, with little immediate capacity to give back. Of course, we still need to give to such needs. It is a cooperative effort for all of us as a responsible society to help people in a dire situation to get back on their feet.

The old adage about teaching a man to fish rather than just feeding him applies very well to this principle of giving.

Here is an example of non-intelligent giving, in which dependency is fostered rather than independence.

> *John has always been a strong individual and also a solo player. He owns his own realty company and feels that he can do his job better than anyone else can. After 30 years, however, he is getting tired because he rarely gets a vacation and would like some time off.*
>
> *Finally, he reluctantly hires Pete to run his company so he can take some time off. Unfortunately he will not delegate key tasks to Pete. He believes Pete won't do a good job. When he gives Pete a major task to do, he ends up taking over anyway and doing it himself. Pete often sits around with little to do and is unhappy that he is not getting the training or opportunity he was promised.*
>
> *One day John decides to take a two-week vacation even though he really hasn't trained Pete properly to do his job. Pete cannot do the job successfully because John was doing all the major functions for him. Pete realizes he is completely dependent on John, and starts to panic. He calls John and interrupts his vacation. John is enraged that he has to cut his vacation short. He fires Pete and goes back to running the company himself.*

The following, on the other hand, illustrates the value of giving something back.

Belinda spends a few hours a week doing volunteer work with senior citizens in a nursing home. She primarily spends time with one lady, Judy, who has no family or friends visiting her. Judy is lonely and depressed, and frequently secludes herself. Belinda talks with her, goes to lunch with her, reads to her, and takes walks with her.

Belinda notices that Judy has improved, but is still somewhat depressed. Judy used to contribute her time and energy to helping others before she got into the nursing home. In the nursing home, she is not encouraged to contribute. Missing the feeling of being of value, Judy generally feels depressed.

Belinda decides that the best way she can help Judy is to help her contribute to others. She finds out that Judy used to play the violin and that she can still can play many beautiful melodies. Belinda helps Judy acquire a violin. Judy now plays for the residents of the nursing home. At group gatherings or private visits in the rooms of her friends, she shares her gift of music. In this way, both Belinda and Judy have enriched the lives of many people.

To be able to inspire others to reciprocate is a priceless skill that creates self-sufficiency, purpose, confidence, trust, and happiness – all great qualities to be shared and multiplied in The Giving Zone.

CHAPTER 22 EXERCISE

It is important to take a look at possible situations in our lives where we may be taking and giving little back in return. The purpose of this exercise is to spot situations in which we are receiving much in value and yet not giving much in return.

1. Is there someone in your life with whom who you feel that the giving is out of balance – you receive quite freely, but you give back little in return?

2. How can you give more intelligently – what can you give back to balance the giving so that you give back equitably?

3. What would be the consequences of both of you giving intelligently (both giving and receiving equitably)? Keep writing consequences (results) until you have a realization of something important that gives you a deeper insight.

4. Repeat 1. to 3. over and over until you have a noticeable shift in your awareness.

CHAPTER 23

USING MONEY WITH WISDOM

"When I chased after money, I never had enough. When I got my life on purpose and focused on giving of myself and every-thing that arrived into my life, then I was prosperous."
—Wayne Dyer

Money seems to be an ever-present part of our lives. Nearly all of us are participants in the world of money. It's needed for so many things we are involved with on a daily basis. How we handle money is a very important aspect of our lives. They say that "love makes the world go around." But, it takes money to go around the world.

There is a tremendous connection between our character and how we use money. People of lower character will tend not to use money wisely. People of high character will tend to use it wisely. How does this relate to the process of giving? Those who are of strong character will tend to give money to contribute to the lives of others, and they will also tend to have money – savings, invest-ments, etc.

Those who are lower in character will tend not to contribute money and will tend to spend more than they earn. They have great difficulty in deferring gratification.

Best-selling author of *Rich Dad Poor Dad* Robert Kiyosaki shares that stress around money is one of the strongest stresses there is. He encourages each of us to develop "financial intelligence" so that we can develop the kind of lifestyle we want, and have financial freedom.

A major part of being intelligent about money is not to spend more than we earn.

Alan Walter talks about "Valuable Money." "Valuable Money" has to do with treating your personal income like a business. You are not so concerned with how much money you earned for the year. Your concern is how much money you have left over at the end of the year.

What you have left over at the end of the year is what you earned.

For example, if we earn $300,000 in a year and spend $350,000 for that year, we earned a –$50,000. A few years like this and we could easily become bankrupt.

If we earn $60,000 for the year and spend $50,000 for the year, we earned +$10,000.

This simple concept changed how I looked at finances and handled them.

As related to the subject of giving, the more we save and invest, the more we have to give, not only to charitable organizations, but also for ourselves. Once we save and invest we can accumulate wealth to help many people and have the lifestyle we desire.

The more we overspend, the poorer we get and we have very little if anything to give.

When it comes down to it, our wealth comes from how much we give, not only monetarily, but also in our careers, hobbies, volunteer work, etc.

I once heard of a wealthy man who gave away 90% of what he earned. Can you imagine how truly wealthy he was? His wealth was not only financial in form, but also came from the satisfaction of all the people he helped.

Bill Gates recently donated four billion dollars to a charity. How would it feel if you had the power to really do that kind of good?

I have also found that developing a positive attitude about money is very important. One problem many people have is that they resent it when they pay for something, especially a bill. They will typically ask something like, "What is the damage?" when it's time to pay for something.

This type of attitude will create lack rather than abundance. It infers that when you pay a bill, to your power company for example, that you have experienced financial damage.

When you have a positive attitude about money, instead, you will gratefully give the money to pay your power bill because you appreciate the service of having electricity for your home. You understand the give and take of life, and therefore you appreciate what you give and what you receive.

Another area connected to money has to do with ethical shortcuts some people take when paying for some items. For example, some people will not buy musical recordings, but will copy them from friends. Another example is people who pirate software. People might think they are saving money, but actually this type of habit is very expensive.

Jerry Clark, a well-known international trainer and speaker, teaches in his tape series "Building on the Shoulders of Giants," that people who make copies of recordings instead of paying for them have poverty consciousness. Such people think there isn't enough, so they take from others who make their living from that recording.

Most important, what goes around comes around. An attitude of lack and an action of lack will result in poverty – not only monetarily, but also in emotional, mental, and spiritual lack.

Creating abundance is natural. Remember, if we are not getting what we want, it is likely that we are operating according to a hidden agenda. Thus, people who use ethical shortcuts may think what they want is to have money, but actually, trying to get away with it and not get caught may be what they really want. This hidden agenda could be more important than having money. Their focus is not really on making money. The result is that they are broke.

Remember, Alan Walter said:

For something to happen, someone has to make it happen.

Thus, a person who is broke is working to be broke – it's usually done unconsciously.

Those who are strong financially, achieving their success and family goals, etc. are working directly to accomplish these positive outcomes.

There is much merit and freedom from having the financial abundance wanted to acquire the things needed for achieving our purposes and goals.

Wallace D. Wattles says in *Science of Being Rich*:

> Success in life is becoming what you want to be; you can become what you want to be only by making use of things, and you can have the free use of things only as you become rich enough to buy them.... The man who has nothing to give cannot fill his place as a husband/or father, as a citizen, or as a man.

The more wealth we obtain, the more we can give to others as well as to ourselves. For example, the rich person can set up foundations to give fortunes to charities. The rich person can provide jobs for hundreds or even thousands of people. People who are wealthy can improve the quality of life for many of us. Bill Gates, for example, has improved our lives significantly through his contribution in the computer and software world.

Wattles teaches that there is enough abundance on the planet for everyone to be rich. He also stresses that the study of becoming rich is a noble and most necessary one, and that the key in that study is to develop an ability to direct our thoughts.

The quality of our thinking directly affects the degree to which we are poor or rich. An example of inaccurate thinking is that most people think that they are poor all their lives because of circumstances outside of their control. This is not true. There are many people who start out very poor and become very rich. There are also people who start out wealthy and end up poor.

Alan Walter says:

Poverty does not just happen . . .

He also states that "[i]t takes just as much work to be poor as it does to be rich."

> *I learned years ago that my thoughts as well as my actions dictated the amount of wealth I achieved. In the past I had negative thinking when it came to wealth. One area of negative thinking was my attitude toward very wealthy and powerful people. I was prejudiced toward them and didn't trust them. This attitude contributed to keeping me far away from wealth.*
>
> *I also did not take the necessary steps to become wealthy. I did not do what wealthy people did. For example, I lacked clear goals, and had mediocre plans and actions.*
>
> *As I changed my thoughts and actions to positive and productive ones, and modeled myself after wealthy people, my financial picture improved.*

Alan Walter shares that there are certain things people do to make sure they are poor:

1. "Do not communicate to anyone who would help you prosper."

2. "...complain about how underpaid, how unhappy and mistreated you are and how bad your life really is."

3. "Make sure you do not take your next step in life."

4. "Never set any goals."

After studying this important material of Mr. Walter, in my own words here are some additional things people do to make sure they are poor.

5.   Be prejudiced against, critical of, and unfriendly toward wealthy people; assume that wealthy people are dishonest, crooked, non-caring, manipulative, and bad, etc.

6.   Stay away from powerful and wealthy people. Make sure that you surround yourself only with people who are broke and not successful.

7.   Blame wealthy and powerful people for your circumstances and be sure to communicate your dissatisfaction with them to others.

8.   Resent that you owe money, be late on your bills or do not pay them at all. Be sure to accumulate more and more bad debt. Do not keep your promises.

9.   Waste time on unimportant tasks such as watching TV.

10.   When you have a problem, do not look at what you are doing to create it.

11.   When you visualize your future, make sure that you see disappointing outcomes.

If you do the above steps, you will reap poverty.

When we take the steps to be poor, we fall into what Alan Walter calls "The House of Mirrors Trap." This is living in an existence of not actually seeing what is in front of us. We perceive based on our inner mirror that projects distorted or false realities about people and circumstances. It is a reality that superimposes on everyone, "It has nothing to do with me." This can produce very destructive consequences in our relationships and in our careers.

An example of "The House of Mirrors Trap" is that some people may have the prejudgment that wealthy people are greedy. This is a generalization and it is false.

Others may think that wealthy people are non-caring. This is also a generalization and it is also false.

Our prejudices toward others are embedded in "The House of Mirrors" inside each of us.

If you wish to break out of your "House of Mirrors Trap," one important step is to find out what you are doing that is similar to what you are critical of in others. For the purpose of this chapter look at the similar behavior you have compared to the very actions for which you criticize powerful and wealthy people.

For example, I used to have the generalization and prejudice that wealthy people are manipulative. The truth was that I was manipulative toward others in my life. My "House of Mirrors Trap" projected my undesirable behavior onto wealthy people. It had nothing to do with them. It was a false reality of mine.

Let's now look at eleven things that people do that tend to make them wealthy.

1. Make a habit of talking with people who could really help you prosper.

2. Know that you get back what you put out. The monetary rewards, your treatment, and the quality of life you receive are dependent on what you are giving.

3. Keep taking your next step in life.

4. Set goals and form plans.

5. Do not be prejudiced against people, whether they are poor or wealthy. Judge people based on their individual merit and character.

6. Find successful and wealthy people and spend time with them. Be willing to learn from them and put into action

their recommendations that could help you advance.

7.   Appreciate how certain successful and powerful people have helped you in your life – given you a job, and an income, and believed in you when others did not believe in you.

8.   Have gratitude for the services and products you use, and pay for them. Pay all bills on time. Get ahead financially. Keep your promises.

9.   Spend much of your spare time advancing your skills and talents – in taking classes, developing hobbies, creating new income sources, sharing meaningful time with family and friends, and taking time to plan and contemplate.

10. When you have a problem, first look at what you are doing to cause the problem. Then see if others are doing something to cause that problem too.

11. When you visualize your future, see yourself having successful outcomes.

If you do the above steps, you are taking positive steps toward building wealth.

Do the following wealth-building exercise when you find yourself having a prejudiced reaction to powerful and wealthy people. Of course this is also a valuable exercise for helping you let go of prejudice or undue criticism toward any type of person. The following exercise is also contained in Chapter 31, *Being Loving*:

1.   **What do I prejudge or dislike in another person?**

2.   **Tell me about that.**

3.   **Have you ever done that very thing, or something similar?**

4.   **If so, what have been the consequences (results)? List the consequences until you've had a realization of something important that gives you a deeper understanding.**

The financial world that we experience is created and directed by our thoughts. Our attitude, skills, and ethical habits determine the financial outcomes we have. When money is used for the good, it is a powerful tool that we can use to contribute toward a better life, a better family, a better society, and a better world.

If you did not do the above exercise because you feel you have no prejudices toward wealthy and powerful people, it is especially recommended that you do the exercise that follows.

CHAPTER 23 EXERCISE

The purpose of this exercise is to become aware of negative attitudes about money and help shift any possible negative attitudes to the positive.

1.   Make a list of any negative attitudes you may have about money. Reviewing this chapter may be helpful in spotting possible negative attitudes.

2.   Select one negative attitude from your list and write down the consequences for having that negative attitude. Keep writing consequences until you've had a realization of something important that gives you a deeper insight.

3.   Write down ways you could change that attitude. (Example: "There isn't enough." This attitude can be changed by looking at what you *do* have in your life and expressing gratitude for it.)

4.   Repeat 2. and 3. over and over until you experience a noticeable shift in your awareness.

CHAPTER 24

THRIVING IN THE WORLD OF BUSINESS AND SALES

"When one door closes another door opens;
but we so often look so long and so regretfully upon
the closed door, that we do not see the ones which open for us."
—Alexander Graham Bell

The topic of business and sales is at the heart of The Giving Zone because those businesspeople who have a great propensity to give fully to their customers will tend to thrive in their business and make a lot of customers happy. Since nearly all of us interface with businesspeople frequently or are businesspeople ourselves, this topic is very central to this book.

For the purpose of this chapter, a businessperson is someone who is a business owner, business executive, sales manager, customer-service worker or someone in another role connected to serving customers.

It is very likely that if you're reading this book, you already have some awareness of how important it is to have a giving attitude as a central focus connected to business and sales. The purpose of this chapter is to help you recognize the degree of giving you observe in the businesspeople and salespeople with whom you do business. Businesspeople and salespeople who are very giving in nature tend to be more honest and will most likely have better products for us to choose from.

For those of you in business or sales, this chapter can give you a greater awareness of how to enhance the amount of giving you have while conducting your own particular business and sales activities.

Also some of the readers of this book are business owners or sales managers who oversee other businesspeople and salespeople. If you can become more aware of the degree to which your people are giving, you can make a big difference in the success of your company. Some of the characteristics of those who are not giving can be very subtle; yet, if you learn to spot these traits in the people who work for you, your business success can increase.

I have had some powerful lessons in the area of business and sales. Remember, I have had many opportunities to learn from my mistakes. Quite a few years ago, when I first was introduced to sales, I was not as strongly focused on the customers' needs as I should have been. I was too centered on getting what I wanted.

My experiences in sales at the time were painful – rejection, disappointment, loss of self-respect, and some failure. This is because my prospective customers could tell that I wasn't strongly interested in their needs. As I learned to focus on truly giving to the customer, sales became a more fun and enhancing experience for both the customer and myself.

Recently, I hired a time-management expert to help me with organization. He came to my house and worked with me for a couple of hours to help get me started. He was completely of service and had one of the most helpful attitudes of anyone I've ever met.

Actually, his attitude of serving the client was so pleasantly powerful that it nearly bowled me over, and it has left a very strong impression in my mind. I cannot help but refer people to him. He genuinely wants to help.

This giving attitude in business is the polar opposite of what some businesspeople, particularly salespeople, practice – instead they try to get whatever they can from their customers. Typically these salespeople want to make the big sale. If they don't make the big sale they're disappointed and will let the prospective customer know they're disappointed. This is an attempt to intimidate the customer to buy. A pillage-and-plunder sales method may make a few sales, but it also results in lots of adversaries.

Such salespeople are concerned with what they can get, not on helping customers get what they want. This is a violation of what it actually takes to be prosperous.

Your prosperity is a result of what you give, not what you take. The key to doing business and sales is to help customers get what they want.

The consequences of using an attitude of taking from the customer rather than giving are numerous: Many clients will have buyer's remorse and ask for their money back. The salesperson will experience the loss of friends and potential friends. Also there is the inevitability of facing the hostility of some unhappy customers.

In addition, lowered self-esteem results from using and hurting customers – selling them something they don't want, the use of pressure and intimidation, charging more than the product is worth, etc. People who use other people pay a terrible price. Most will tend to feel a sense of guilt and remorse, which causes lowered self-worth.

Lowered self-worth automatically results in lowered success. Each of us has only what we feel we are worthy of having.

Salespeople such as this waste a most precious resource – people. They don't value others, but degrade them. For such a salesperson, the customer is a *thing* to misuse, not a fellow *human being* to respect and care for. One of the worst demonstrations of such an attitude is the salesperson who brags to his cohorts about how much he was able to get away with in selling to the customer.

Remember, some of the characteristics of those businesspeople and salespeople who are not giving can be very subtle. Whether you are a potential customer, or a business owner, carefully observe not only the words used by salespeople, but also look at their attitude. Their language could make it seem that they have a giving disposition, when their attitude is actually one of taking. For example, you may spot something in their tone which is disingenuous – perhaps a sleazy or cold feeling you get about them. It could be a weak, insincere handshake, or a total lack of eye contact. Maybe you feel pressured, manipulated, or conned. You may feel repelled and want to escape. If you do purchase something, you feel like it was more their decision for you to buy, not so strongly your own decision to buy. Pay attention to all of these signals.

Really listen to your intuitive feelings – also known as gut feelings. They are there for a purpose. When we cultivate an intuitive awareness, we have an invaluable tool that protects us, and it can also greatly enhance our success in life.

We get a completely different feeling from the attitude of honest, giving salespeople. There is a warmth, a smile, and a sincere, caring tone in their voice. You feel that there is a genuine interest in you and what you want. Instead of pressure or manipulation, you experience permission to buy or not to buy. Rather than being turned off, you are attracted to converse with this type of salesperson. You made the decision to buy; it was not the salesperson's decision.

There are many benefits for businesspeople and salespeople who operate in the realm of The Giving Zone by being of total service their customers. They'll make many friends, have a clean conscience, enjoy a good reputation, receive numerous referrals, and experience a lot of prosperity and happiness.

The following is a list of some good principles of businesspeople and salespeople who operate in The Giving Zone:

1. Help customers get what they want even if it isn't your product. For example, a customer wants to buy a coat that the particular store doesn't carry. The salesperson refers the customer to a competitor that carries that specific brand. This is being of service to the customer and will leave a favorable impression.

2. Give something back to all potential customers for their time. When you approach potential customers, you are taking some of their time. Therefore, give something back. It could be a smile, some helpful information, some words of encouragement, etc.

3. Always maintain the posture of helping customers get what they want, not what you want.

4. Work toward building a relationship of trust. This is more important than trying to force a sale. Your character and reputation are far more important than the sale.

5. Help educate the customer to make intelligent buying decisions and to get their best use of the product.

6. Especially concerning costly items such as group accounts, or commercial real estate, it's often best to have more than one meeting to make the sale. The first meeting may be set up just to share information and get acquainted.

7. Sales language involves terms that encourage buying rather than being sold. For example, "Let me see if I can help you." Rather than, "You need to get this today or you'll lose out."

8. You always give customers an out. This means that you give them permission not to buy, which relieves pressure and makes it easier for them to say yes. For example, you can say, "If we do business, it will be because you will get something you will be happy with."

9. On bigger items, you make it a practice to stay in contact with the customer after the sale is made. You make a phone call or come out to visit the customer to see that everything is OK. This also is a perfect opportunity to ask for referrals, because happy customers are likely to be the most excited when first getting the product and will probably want their friends to know about it.

Actually, each of these nine principles helps with getting referrals – because you are helping the customer, and that means that the customer is likely to want to help you.

Businesspeople and salespeople who follow principles of The Giving Zone will be very successful. Their customers will tend to be repeat customers, and will eagerly refer their friends. It's about following the Golden Rule and playing win-win in life. Business is a key part of our life. Good business means a better life for all of us and ultimately a better world.

CHAPTER 24 EXERCISE

The purpose of this exercise is to help customers, salespeople, and businesspeople to have greater success in their experiences in the business world.

1. As a customer, begin observing salespeople to see if their approach tends toward taking from the customer or giving to the customer. Use the tips in this chapter and particularly listen to your intuition concerning their attitude.

2. If you are a salesperson, make a plan of how you can increase your abilities to work in The Giving Zone. Study the principles outlined in this chapter.

3. If you are a sales manager or a business owner with salespeople, carefully observe your salespeople to see if their approach tends toward taking from the customer or giving to the customer. Study the pointers in this chapter. In addition, concerning your salespeople, look at the results they are getting in their sales as an indicator. For example, if a salesperson has low sales volume, customer complaints, reports of buyer's remorse from customers, shows up late to work, is absent from work too often, or shows a poor attitude, your salesperson may be tending toward the taking side in working with customers. This is not always the case, but it is worth considering.

CHAPTER 25

BEING INTERESTED IN OTHERS

"In everyone's life, at some time, our inner fire goes out.
It is then burst into flame by an encounter with another human
being. We should all be thankful for those people who rekindle
the inner spirit."
—Albert Schweitzer

*T*he gift of finding out what people are interested in is a powerful key to connecting to others, and a core communication skill for living in The Giving Zone.

The feeling of satisfaction that comes from good conversation is largely a result of identifying the interests of other people and communicating along the lines of these interests. This is pivotal to the process of making friends. Many people live lives of loneliness because they don't seem to be able to truly connect to anyone in a meaningful way. The years pass by and they may become more and more isolated.

As mentioned in Chapter 10, one major problem that numerous people have is that they do not know how to hold a conversation. They tend to talk about themselves and do very little listening.

Does a connection occur by talking about yourself? Usually not, unless the person you are talking with asks you questions and wants to know about you.

Actually, it is the asking of questions that connects us. Along with asking questions is the ability to listen. Many people think they have to talk a lot in order to hold a conversation; they will go through an entire conversation without finding out anything about the other person. Or worse, if the other person can even get a word in, the incessant talker won't even show any interest in the other person.

The great listener is a powerful conversationalist and connector, a master of asking questions. The listener with the right questions will make the other person feel very important and special. You give others a priceless gift when you truly listen to them. It is a process that superb leaders, salespeople, consultants, and parents understand.

A question which gets people to talk about their interests is pivotal in fostering connection and friendship. Questions that really help us connect to other people are:

"What are your interests?"

"What do you like to do?"

"What kind of work do you do?"

Another question that draws out interests is:

"What do you really want in your life?"

When you get people to talk about their interests and desires, they are likely to think that you are a very interesting person. The best conversationalists are those who ask key questions and say very little.

Once you open the door to finding out about others' interests and desires, you will develop new friends and create better friendships with the people you know.

My wife and I visited Hawaii after not having been there for quite a few years. We had previously lived there for 13 years and had some friends who still resided there. Upon our visit we got together with 11 different people. With each of them, we listened as they caught us up with their lives and conversed about their interests. We asked questions and said very little. We were amazed at how close we got.

Really, the simple question which gets people to come to life is:

"What kinds of things are you interested in?" or "What do you like to do?"

A person may be feeling discouraged. If you show a genuine interest, that person is likely to start remembering key interests and aspirations. Color even returns to the person's face. People who are listened to in a conversation become excited and animated.

Frank Bettger in his book, *How I Raised Myself From Failure to Success in Selling*, shares a question that he used, which helped him make big sales. Mr. Bettger would ask:

"How did you get started in the building construction business [or whatever business the person was in]?"

Frank Bettger asked this question and listened to one prospect's life story for three hours. The prospect shared key interests and felt understood and cared about. He also purchased a very large order of Frank Bettger's service.

When we ask people about how they got started in their career and allow them to describe the years of their career journey, they will often become very excited and animated. Hardly anyone ever asks such a core question. Asking the question shows a deep interest in others. They'll feel very appreciated as they open up about their successes and the obstacles they experienced along the way.

Ask people questions about their interests and desires, and you will be offering them a valuable gift. If you will make the time, ask people to tell you how they got started in their career. Active listening along the lines of others' interests brings them to life, creates strong connections, and much joy. This is a great description of the perfect flow of communication that takes place in The Giving Zone. Communicating along these lines will bring people to life. They will most likely genuinely listen to you, too, along with a renewed interest in you.

CHAPTER 25 EXERCISE

The purpose of this exercise is to increase your ability to show sincere interest in other people.

1. As you meet new people ask a question around their interests such as: What do you do? What do you do for fun? What are you particularly interested in? What are your other interests? Really listen to their answers with genuine interest and ask more questions along the lines of what really interests them.

2. When you can have more time with someone, ask, "How did you get started in _____ (whatever his or her career is)? Be prepared to listen with great interest for up to a couple of hours or so and you will make a new friend.

CHAPTER 26

GIVING APPRECIATION

"A great man is always willing to be little."
—Ralph Waldo Emerson

If you want to win people over, show genuine appreciation. Most people melt when they are appreciated. Appreciation is a gift that virtually everyone wants to receive. It is one of the most predominant types of communication we can share in The Giving Zone.

However, most people resist sharing their appreciation for each other. Instead they will freely share their criticism and will withhold what many people want the most – appreciation.

Appreciation is a healing gift that can transform lives.

Some research has shown that on the job, people want recognition more than they want pay increases.

Interestingly enough, many people do not have appreciation for themselves. If you do not appreciate yourself, you will probably have difficulty appreciating others. Have you ever heard someone say, "I'm getting too much appreciation"? Probably not. Instead, we are typically more likely to hear comments such as:

"I work so hard, and the only thing my boss comments on is

what I do wrong."

or

"I give my employees extra time off, I give them every consideration, and I never hear a simple thank-you from them."

Keep the following statement in mind when you are communicating to the people in your life:

A little appreciation goes a long way.

Many people are reluctant to express appreciation. Part of a reluctance to show appreciation stems from a culture in which we are perfection-oriented. This perfectionism is rooted in the school as well as in the home:

"It's got to be just right to be acceptable."

"If it's not perfect, it's no good."

"I just never find it good enough for me."

If we are perfectionists, we will tend to give very little appreciation. Nothing is ever good enough for us.

> When I was in college, I had a part-time job as a draftsman. My boss was a very intelligent and capable man, but he was a perfectionist who rarely gave compliments. I worked very hard to produce drawings that were nearly perfect.
> One day I produced a drawing in which I could not detect any mistakes. (This was the late sixties when things were hand-drawn. The advent of computer drawings hadn't arrived.) I showed the perfect drawing to my boss and he said, "There is an imperfection in the paper." He found nothing wrong with my drawing, but he had found a flaw

in the paper. Sure enough, there was a tiny imperfection in the paper itself. I actually took it as a compliment because it was the most positive comment from him that I had ever received on any drawing I had ever completed. At least I was able to turn it around and discover the appreciation hidden in his comment.

The other side of the coin is that some people have difficulty in accepting any appreciation they are given.

Deborah is told by Phil, a work associate, that she does a great job in customer service. Deborah says, "Oh it's not that great, I could be doing better." How does Phil feel when Deborah cannot accept this appreciation? He probably feels a bit slighted. An expression of appreciation is a gift. To not accept it is like turning down a wrapped gift someone wants to give you.

This non-acceptance of appreciation short-circuits the cycle of reciprocation. The result is likely to be a painful emotion – a rejection or loss for the person who tried to give the compliment.

Another cause of non-appreciation comes from the belief that you should only give appreciation if someone does a superb job. In fact, appreciation is most needed when someone is struggling and failing. People need encouragement.

The following is a story told by Dr. Dreikurs, MD, author of *Children the Challenge*:

Billy is learning to write longhand. He is struggling to get the letters right and is way behind the other students in the class. The teacher looks at the paper and can hardly read anything on it. Billy is told by the teacher that the paper is a terrible mess. She then proceeds to humiliate Billy further by taking the paper, tearing it into bits and throwing the pieces up into the air. Billy is devastated.

His teacher continues to humiliate Billy for poor hand-

writing throughout the rest of the school year and Billy's handwriting does not improve. What's worse is that Billy's self-esteem deteriorates.

The new school year arrives and Billy has a new teacher. The teacher asks everyone to write some sentences in longhand.

Billy writes out his sentences and he is terrified that this new teacher will again humiliate him because his writing is illegible. The teacher comes over, looks at Billy's handwriting and sees that it is very difficult to read.

However, the teacher finds one good letter which is written well and says, "You really drew this g well. Would you please draw another g?"

Through appreciation and encouragement, Billy's handwriting vastly improves. But, even more important, his self-esteem also improves.

The master of appreciation will give appreciation when no one else will, and offer a magic phrase that can turn someone's life around: The magic is in the use of encouragement and appreciation.

Many people do the opposite – they hurt other people through using harsh criticism and discouragement. There is an expression that has been around for a long time:

"The knife is not at the side, it is at the tip of the tongue."

Have you ever been discouraged, and someone came by and said something of appreciation or encouragement to you? What would happen if whenever we found people who are discouraged, we shared words of appreciation and encouragement to them? It will have very positive effects.

Some people have a spouse or partner who hardly ever shares words of appreciation. How do you feel when you are around someone who does not share words of appreciation?

> *My wife is great at handling this problem. One day my wife had done something for me that was quite difficult and took quite a bit of effort. I forgot to thank her. She said, "How about giving me a thank-you. That's all I want." I felt embarrassed for not thanking her and promptly expressed my appreciation. At that moment I felt such enormous appreciation towards her. And it came from her asking me for it.*

Often in marriages, the individuals will hesitate to ask for what they want. They expect the other person to know what they want automatically. Yet, in some cases people can wait for years and the other person doesn't give them what they want. They are missing the boat; all they need to do is ask for what they want. Some people are oblivious to the gift of appreciation. Some aren't aware that the only comments they share are critical ones. Some people also aren't aware that they continually take from others and give very little back.

Many of us make the costly mistake of assuming that other people who have these problems are aware of them. Yet they may be acting in ignorance. And it's as if we expect them to read our minds.

It is OK to let the people in our lives know when they are doing something that is causing a problem. Not to tell them keeps our relationships in the dark. Lack of communication harms relationships. Opening up the doors to communication enhances and strengthens relationships. Communication is fundamental to the giving process and to succeeding happily in The Giving Zone.

The sharing of our appreciation is one of the most important and powerful forms of communication we possess. It's a gift that can create miracles in many people's lives. Give it freely and others will start to give it back to you freely. Be generous with the gift of appreciation. It is like spreading fairy dust to create magic in all the lives it touches. Appreciation gives hope, opens hearts, and brings about inspiration and joy. Use this outstanding positive process frequently. People are yearning for it.

CHAPTER 26 EXERCISES

Many people have the habit of seeing what's wrong with others and not appreciating the positive side of the individual. This exercise is to help develop awareness of what we can appreciate in others as well as in ourselves.

EXERCISE ONE

1. Choose someone you could appreciate more.

2. Make a list of qualities you could appreciate in that person. Keep listing these qualities until you have a realization of something important that gives you a deeper insight.

3. Repeat 1. and 2. over and over until you experience a shift in your awareness.

EXERCISE TWO

1. Make a list of qualities you can appreciate in yourself. Keep writing down these qualities until you experience a shift in your awareness.

CHAPTER 27

EXPRESSING GRATITUDE

"Heaven means to be one with God"
—Confucius

T here are many measures of wealth besides money. Having good friends is a measure of wealth. Having activities that you love to do, including both work and leisure, can be considered a measure of wealth.

An essential measure of wealth is the amount of gratitude we have.

So many people are continually miserable because they feel lacking in what they have and hardly ever feel fulfilled. Even if they have good health, good finances, good friends, etc., they are always unhappy because they feel they don't have enough of whatever it is that they want. They are ungrateful for what they do have – a negative process that causes emptiness and lack, which will restrain success.

The ability to cultivate gratitude is indispensable to one's happiness and well-being. We all have the ability to feel grateful for what we have achieved in life, for the family and friendships we have, and for what we have achieved materially.

When we express our gratitude for others it will melt hearts and deepen friendships. This gratitude will naturally spread outward from those who receive it to others who will in turn share their gratitude, and so on. This flow of gratitude is a key ingredient to the creation of a supportive climate in The Giving Zone.

There are many benefits to feeling and expressing gratitude. One of the benefits is that those who cultivate gratitude will tend to have greater enjoyment in life, regardless of their financial situation or whatever circumstances they are experiencing.

Another benefit of gratitude is that it gives us a sense of being in the moment. When we have little or no gratitude, it is difficult to enjoy the moment. We hold onto regrets over what we lack, which tends to keep us living in the past. On the other hand, we can also become obsessive about the future, regretting what we still don't have, which again prevents us from enjoying the moment.

People who don't have gratitude for what they have will tend to feel that they are always lacking. They are wanting more and more and will continue to feel empty inside.

Paul is a business owner who has achieved many measures of success – a large, beautiful luxury home, luxury cars, and a big bank account. He is never satisfied. Continually measuring himself against other wealthier people, he strives to accumulate more and more wealth, rarely having a moment to enjoy what he has achieved.

He spends little time with his family. Instead he works long hours to increase his financial wealth. He is a classic type A personality, never really satisfied with his achievements.

The stress in his life is almost unbearable and nothing he achieves is ever good enough. The few times he sits down with his family at dinner, work is on his mind and he cannot seem to arrive in the moment to really be with his family.

For Paul, the concept of gratitude is foreign. He considers gratitude a waste of time. Yet the price he pays is very large. Tension headaches, a spastic colon, a conflicted marriage, and continual unhappiness are the fruits he reaps.

Julie is also successful in a material sense. As a buyer for a large clothing company, she has achieved many comforts. However, she has gratitude for what she has attained in life as well as gratitude for the simple pleasures in life.

She has cultivated a deep sense of appreciation for her possessions, her family, friends, hobbies, and the liberal travel schedule she enjoys.

She has no problem appreciating the simple pleasures in life. Going out in her rose garden, she can smell a rose, admire its beauty, gaze at the sunset and be in great joy. When she is with family and friends, she communicates with great warmth, appreciation, and satisfaction.

Tammy is someone of low economic means I knew when I lived in Eugene, Oregon. She had a husband, three children, and a simple home. She always emanated gratitude from deep inside. She did this with a warm glowing smile that touched nearly everyone she met.

When she communicated, she would naturally express gratitude for life, for the beauty of the world, and for the people she loved. Even though she didn't have much in the way of finances, she was wealthy in her loving presence, her deep appreciation for beauty, and a steadfast peace of mind.

To have gratitude means to have the ability to complete the activities of life. To really have something, we need to have gratitude for it.

There are a series of steps necessary to attain any goal in life. These include a perception of what we desire, a vision of our completed goal, a plan, and then the implementation of each of the steps.

Once the goal is realized, there is one last essential step, which is celebration — or gratitude — for the accomplishment.

Without gratitude, the goal can never really be complete. This is because the gratitude step implies that you are happy with your accomplishment. And if you are not, then in reality you are still holding the goal as incomplete. You've decided that it is not quite right or not good enough. There is something in your mind that you feel is unfinished. But if you can really feel gratitude instead, you free yourself to go on to your next accomplishment.

> *One personal example is the gratitude I have for my wife. I feel that she is the greatest woman in the world. I am also very fortunate that she has quite a bit of gratitude toward me. This gratitude is a completion step for what we've attained in our marriage thus far. And it is a core part of our love for each other. If we did not have gratitude towards each other, I believe we would have a very weak connection and a meaningless, superficial relationship.*
>
> *My wife and I are also continually growing in our shared goals as well as in our individual goals. Thus we are creating new areas where we can share gratitude toward each other as we achieve our goals.*

We need to have gratitude each step of the way in the attainment of a goal, not just for its completion. We can feel gratitude for embarking on a new goal, for example. We can also have gratitude for having set plans for the attainment of that goal. And we can express gratitude for each small accomplishment along the way.

To not have gratitude for the people in our lives will cause us to be more negative in our dealings with them. They will tend to be pulled down by us and drained by us.

There are many activities that tend to sap our ability to feel gratitude. Addictions – too much TV, too much food, toxic diets, drugs, alcohol, criticism, blame, etc. – keep us distracted from all that we have to be grateful for.

Overcoming addictions can be one way to help us experience gratitude as well as many other positive characteristics. However, there are situations in which we are unable to overcome addictions on our own. In this case it is very important to seek expertise – consulting, training, etc.

There are activities that we can engage in that build and increase gratitude – communicating on a meaningful level, spiritual pursuits, increasing our knowledge, doing volunteer work, joining team activities, creating or enjoying art, music, etc.

Cultivating gratitude is a gift that nurtures not only ourselves, but also everyone around us. Gratitude is a measure of true wealth, success, and happiness, and it is one of the wonderful attributes that enhances our living in The Giving Zone.

CHAPTER 27 EXERCISE

The gratitude we cultivate is a measure of wealth. This exercise will help increase the amount of gratitude you have.

1. Make a list of people, groups, organizations, situations, etc. that you want to have more gratitude for.

2. Pick one item from the list and write down the things you could have gratitude for connected to that item. Keep writing these things connected to this one item until you've had a realization of something important that gives you a deeper insight.

3. Repeat 2. over and over until you've had a noticeable shift in your awareness of how much you have to be grateful for.

CHAPTER 28

BEING ABLE TO FORGIVE

*"Your work is to discover your world and
then with all your heart give yourself to it."*
—Buddha

Many people harbor anger, resentment, or even hatred toward a family member, friend, or associate – or sometimes even toward someone they hardly know. This animosity may last many years and occasionally will last a lifetime. To not forgive someone can feel like a knife cutting away at the heart; the pain can be at times unbearable.

Those who have a forgiving heart find easy entrance into The Giving Zone. Forgiveness and the ability to give work hand in hand because forgiveness in and of itself is a giving act.

Why do people not forgive others? One cause of unforgivingness is that people who refuse to forgive will decide that they are "right" in not forgiving, and will continue to justify their unforgivingness. I have witnessed many heartbreaking situations in which a parent will not forgive a child or a child will not forgive a parent. The person who usually hurts most from this unforgivingness is actually the one who won't forgive. Thus, a profound gift we can give to ourselves as well as to others is the act of forgiveness.

I know this first-hand because I have previously been guilty of choosing not to forgive. There were individuals in my life that I hadn't forgiven for years. The consequences of my unforgivingness became dire for me. I endured tremendous physical stress and deep emotional pain, and got off track in fulfilling my purpose in my life. I paid a big price, wasting vast amounts of time – and I was absent much of the time from The Giving Zone.

When we don't forgive, we stay stuck in the past. We cannot be present in the moment. To not be in the moment makes life barren, with little joy.

My wife suffered during the years that I was guilty of not forgiving others. Because I held onto my unforgivingness, there were many times she found me to be emotionally draining during these years.

The key to understanding forgiveness of those we feel have wronged us has to do with being able to forgive ourselves. When we cannot forgive another person, especially when years have passed by, there is almost certainly something inside of us as well, for which we feel we cannot forgive. Thus the major key to being able to forgive others has to do with being able to forgive ourselves first.

For example, Mary could not forgive her 16-year-old daughter for getting in trouble with some adolescents at her school. Her daughter was prosecuted for vandalism and drinking under age. The arrest was in the newspapers and Mary was filled with shame, embarrassment, and anger. She felt violated.

It was now two years since Mary had virtually turned her back on her daughter. The two of them were like ships passing in the night, with hardly a word spoken between them. The unhappiness in the house was so thick, you could practically feel it when you walked inside.

One day Mary decided to see a professional coach to help her. She felt that her bitterness was destroying their lives. After a few sessions, it was discovered that Mary herself had gotten in trouble with the law as a 17-year-old for driving under the influence of alcohol.

Mary had been harboring deep feelings of guilt, shame, and regret over this incident. When her own daughter was caught in a similar crime, it unconsciously triggered the self-hatred and regret she had for her own past actions.

Mary was finally able to forgive herself and therefore she could forgive her daughter. One night Mary came home and greeted her daughter with an open heart, and tears of joy. They talked for hours, and Mary told her daughter all about the real cause of her not having forgiven her. It was a very happy reunion. The two of them were close once more and their wounds soon healed; the bond they formed eventually made them inseparable.

When we do not forgive someone, not only does it disconnect us from that person, but it will also tend to weaken our connection to all other people, because of the angry, hateful, and vengeful feelings that we harbor inside us. To not forgive will also weaken our ability to give, and thus will greatly reduce our ability to live in The Giving Zone.

I couldn't forgive a number of people because they seemed to have been verbally abusive. Specifically, they appeared to me to be very critical, harsh, and uncaring.

When I had some personal coaching, I found that the things I could not forgive others for I was in fact guilty of myself. I discovered that I was very critical, harsh, and uncaring at times with some people – thus I myself was verbally abusive. By changing my behavior and forgiving myself for past harmful actions, I was able to forgive the

*others whom I had judged for so long as critical, harsh,
and uncaring. A great weight was lifted from me.*

*Two other things helped me to forgive. The first was a
very deep desire at the core of my soul to forgive. I found
that my lack of forgiveness was tearing me apart inside. I
had to forgive others and I had to forgive myself. This
desire to forgive was one of the strongest passions I'd ever
had in my life.*

*The stronger our passion or desire, the more likely and
quicker the desire will be fulfilled. Of course, desire plus
correct action is pivotal to fulfilling any dream or aspiration.*

*The second thing that helped me forgive was calling on
a Higher Power – my connection to God. I needed that
help and I received it. My life has improved immensely
since I chose to forgive. My wife is much happier with me.
Past relationships have healed and there is increased closeness in my friendships.*

A question naturally arises for those who have experienced
severe abuse, particularly in their childhood. How do you forgive
others in such a situation? This challenge to forgive can be also
compounded by guilt and shame. Even though the guilt and shame
belong to the perpetrator, people who have been abused may often
blame themselves.

This is unfortunate because children, for example, who are
physically abused at a very young age, have done nothing in their
behavior to provoke the perpetrator, yet they may end up blaming
themselves for the abusive acts. In this case, it's important to put
the responsibility for the abusive acts where it belongs – on the
perpetrator. This is an essential step in the forgiveness process.

*Again, I personally have found that it helps to look for
any possible similar abusive traits that I might possibly
have in common with the perpetrator of the abuse. For
example, my stepfather was an alcoholic who was very
abusive verbally. As I mentioned before, I was a verbally
abusive person. When I made great changes to let go of*

my own verbal abusiveness, it was an important step in the direction of forgiving my stepfather.

Many of the people we connect to in our lives possess certain qualities that are also in ourselves, which we don't see. When they act out those qualities we can get quite upset.

An example of this is that my wife and I tend to both be a bit bossy at times, but neither of us likes to be bossed. If my wife is bossy toward me, I get irritated; and if I'm bossy toward her, she gets irritated. We understand that this is a mutual lesson we are working on. We are helping each other become less and less bossy.

This problem is so much improved compared to years ago when I use to over-dominate. By attracting people in my life with similar qualities, I have been greatly reducing this negative trait.

If we develop a heightened awareness, we will discover where the qualities that upset us in our family, friends, and co-workers, are so often a reflection of similar qualities in ourselves.

Sometimes such a quality is only remotely similar. Perhaps it's our child, who hardly ever cleans his or her room. It's a total mess. But, in looking at the reflection, toward our " inner mirror," we realize that we have areas of our life that are messy. Perhaps our closets are a mess, or our tax records are a mess, and it's been very difficult to find things.

There are key people in our lives who act as mirrors, reflecting back what is inside us. That is why we get so upset when they act out these qualities. Such people are marvelous gifts in disguise. We actually attract them to us so that we can be given an opportunity to work through certain negative traits. We often also attract these same people in our lives to bring to our awareness certain positive qualities we have.

Your mirror is your outer world reflecting back to you your inner world. To forgive others is to forgive yourself for something in your own mirror that is also a reflection in their mirror.

An interesting phenomenon can occur where you have difficulty forgiving someone for something that the person didn't really do.

For example, there have been people in my life whom I thought were verbally abusive who really weren't. I was so verbally abusive in my life that I projected my verbal abusiveness onto them. This was particularly a problem with authority figures. If a boss were firm in asking me to take care of a responsibility I was avoiding, I could feel verbally abused. I was wrong in many such situations. I would blame the boss even though it was my fault, and the boss really wasn't being verbally abusive. I created an artificial forgiveness problem – and worse, I created conflicts at work. Again, I solved this problem when I worked on my own verbal abusiveness.

I highly recommend that you read the above two paragraphs several times. Notice that there exists a primary mechanism that can destroy many relationships – the blaming of others for what we ourselves are responsible for doing.

The gift of forgiveness is the gift of moving from the darkness to the light. Forgiveness is a force that heals relationships, nations, and the world. Each act of forgiveness frees the people involved from the shackles of misery, despair, and dishonesty. Those who are freed then liberate those they touch, and the ripple effect goes out to many others who are also released from the shackles that bind their hearts, and so on. This is a powerful key that unlocks the door to living in the Giving Zone.

CHAPTER 28 EXERCISE

The ability to forgive is a supreme ability that makes a better life for all concerned. This exercise can assist you in the process of forgiveness.

1. Is there someone in your life that you have not forgiven?

2. If so, who is that person?

3. What did that person do to you that makes it difficult for you to forgive? Write it down.

4. Write down two or more things you could do that could help you forgive. (Example: Write a letter of forgiveness. You do not have to send the letter.)

5. Write down the consequences (results) of what would happen in your life and the lives of others connected to you if you forgave this person. Keep writing the consequences until you've had a realization of something important that gives you a deeper insight.

6. If there are other people you want to forgive, repeat 1. to 5. over and over until you experience a shift in your awareness.

CHAPTER 29

GIVING A WARM SMILE

"Wherever you go, go with all your heart"
—Confucius

According to Frank Bettger, "a smile and worry simply won't mix…" Thus, a smile is a great asset to give yourself. Also, when you smile at other people and thus encourage them to smile back, it's also just as difficult for them to smile and worry at the same time.

Why do I choose to write about this topic – the ability to cultivate a good smile? It is because I've experienced first-hand the huge difference a good smile has made in my life and also how a good smile greatly improved the lives of other people in attracting friendships, success, money, and happiness.

There are some rare individuals who have a fantastic smile. They have a gift that is invaluable. They have an ability to melt the hearts of the people they touch. This ability is so powerful that it has been a prime asset in helping some people become superstars. A great smile helps people become great directors of stage productions in life that attract very large audiences.

If you already have a good smile, this chapter will help you cultivate a fabulous smile, which will be of great benefit to you and others in your life.

Early on in life, I had a serious disposition, so there were instances in which my frown blocked what I wanted to communicate. I had a particular wake-up call one day when I was communicating concern for someone verbally, but he interpreted me as grim and critical because of my habitual serious expression. It woke me up and I decided that I needed to cultivate a good smile. This problem of mine was limiting me in many areas of success, and thus diminished my ability to live in The Giving Zone.

As we've discussed, life is about the art of exchange, also known as reciprocation. So when you give someone a smile and that person gives you a smile back, you have exchanged something of great value. I have noticed that if I am frustrated or worried, if I put a genuine smile on my face, my mood improves quite a bit. When we spot people in a lower mood and we give them a smile, it can often have the effect of lifting their mood.

There are situations in which we may feel that we are taking up someone's time and we need to give something back. Making a sales presentation is one such example. Many salespeople hesitate to make sales calls because they are concerned that they are taking someone's time and not giving something back. The solution to this problem is for the salesperson to make sure always to give something back to the potential customer.

Even a genuine smile can be of great value to give in exchange for the time that a potential client has given you. Another thing you can give is to be in a good mood to help raise the mood of the other person. As we discussed earlier, the gift of a high mood is contagious.

I remember that my grandfather had a smile that melted everyone's heart. He made many people feel great just by giving them his very warm smile.

A great smile is rare. Those who have one possess a gift easily worth a million dollars. A great smile is something worth cultivating. If you do not have a great smile, practice smiling even when you don't feel like it. And you will find that smiling comes more easily.

Bettger encourages us to develop a genuine smile from deep inside. Discussing his experience in the business world, he said:

"I determined to cultivate a big, happy smile. . . it couldn't be an insincere, commercialized smile. . ."

Bettger went on to describe how he would think about things he was thankful for, to help him generate a smile that came from deep inside. It was then easy for him to smile warmly. He used this process of being thankful before going into a sales interview in order to greet people with a great smile. It made for huge improvements in the business success he achieved.

Because of my glum look, I decided to practice smiling. So, I still practice smiling many times in a week, cultivating a better and better smile. When I put a smile on my face, I notice that my mood shoots up right away. I feel more peaceful and content. Since developing a much better smile, people react differently to me. They connect much more easily and I connect much more easily with them. Smiling has become a part of me – and it is fun, too.

If my mood falls a bit, one of the things I do to raise my mood is to put a smile on my face. I've practiced this for a couple of years and I smile much more easily now.

A smile can melt someone who is an adversary or a potential adversary. If there are people you have been having a conflict with, greet them with a smile and a warm hello. This can help cut through the conflict. They are expecting you to greet them with indifference or hostility. A smile is a disarming surprise that cuts through the conflict. It communicates friendship rather than hostility.

A smile communicates appreciation. It communicates warmth, friendship, and happiness. It says to the other person: Things are well with me and they are well with you, too. A smile invites people into your life. It makes you irresistible. People want to be around other people who smile because a smile is healing to be around.

According to Frank Bettger, there is even a case of a man who saved his own marriage through smiling. On the brink of divorce, he simply smiled when he was around his wife. It helped change his operating basis from one of complaining to one of a positive disposition, and the healing process could begin.

Give people your best smile. A winning smile is a simple gift that will allow us entry into the Giving Zone, and help keep us there.

CHAPTER 29 EXERCISE

The purpose of this exercise is to help you further develop your smile – whether you tend to have a very developed smile already or an uneasy smile.

1. How can you improve your ability to smile? List all the ideas that come to you.

2. Make a plan to practice using at least one of these ideas to help you improve your smile.

3. What would be the consequences (results) of your having a better-developed attractive smile? Write down the consequences until you've had a shift in your awareness.

CHAPTER 30

USING A WARM HANDSHAKE AND GOOD EYE CONTACT

"The most important part of a successful relationship is to find out what the other person wants and help them find the best way to get it."
—Alan C. Walter

*I*t's surprising how quickly a warm handshake and making eye contact will instantly connect you with the people you meet. Just add that warm smile you've been working on, and you will strengthen every connection you make.

Napoleon Hill was in his office when an elderly lady stopped by unexpectedly to sell financial services. Napoleon intended to be courteous, but to get out of the meeting quickly. However, this woman greeted him with a very beautiful smile and an incredibly warm handshake. The greeting was so powerful that Napoleon Hill in fact nearly buckled. Some of his staff members observed that he was so taken aback by this woman that he was practically in her control. He even sat her down in his office chair and listened to her sales presentation as if she were royalty. She ended up making a couple of sales in his office with a couple of staff people.

When first greeting someone, there is hardly anything more powerful than a smile, along with a warm handshake. If you also add direct eye contact, you have an unbeatable formula for winning people over. When you do this you are giving a gift: You are giving the recipients the feeling of being very special, important, and appreciated. People virtually cannot help but to want to connect with you and cooperate with you.

How does it feel to be greeted by someone who has a limp handshake? Or how about a vice grip? Recently, I shook hands with someone whose strong handshake felt like it was nearly going to break my hand. There is a balance needed in the amount of pressure one uses to create an effective handshake.

Some people shake hands by half-heartedly grabbing just the fingers or fingertips, as if they are barely trying to touch you. This type of weak handshake can make an immediate bad impression. A good handshake is one that takes the full hand for a moment and clasps it warmly.

Another vital part of connecting with people is making eye contact. Recently, we had two men clean the carpets in our home. Both introduced themselves by shaking hands when they came in the door. One of them, however, looked away as if I didn't exist. The other one made very good eye contact as he greeted me. Instantly I had much more trust for the man who made very good eye contact.

People who make good eye contact are communicating that they want to be in your presence.

People who make poor eye contact are communicating that they either don't want to be in your presence or they're not sure if they even want to be in the room at all. They show a lack of interest and/or a lack of confidence.

When communicating with someone, lack of eye contact can also mean that the person is elsewhere, not here with you now. For example, if I'm looking at the floor, ceiling or a picture on the wall instead of at the person, it could mean I'm thinking about my next vacation or about the television show I'm going to watch later that evening.

Some people even turn their head nearly sideways when they

introduce themselves. It almost seems like they are wanting to say hello, and yet escape out the door at the same time. We automatically feel a lack of trust toward these people.

When greeting other people, we have the choice of making them feel like a million dollars — or making them feel like they are of no consequence.

To give people a smile, a warm handshake, and direct eye contact is a terrific gift that will welcome you into their presence as a friend, and place you firmly in The Giving Zone. This simple practice is guaranteed to help open doors and create opportunities for you to benefit many people as well as yourself.

CHAPTER 30 EXERCISE

The purpose of this exercise is to help improve the development of a warm handshake, direct eye contact, and a good smile, when greeting people.

1. Form a plan that each time you greet new people, you will give them your best handshake, direct eye contact, and a winning smile.

2. Keep a journal of how greetings go, and how you can improve. For example, you greet someone new, and in your journal you write: My handshake was warm and confident. I had a very good smile. Next time I need to have better eye contact; I didn't keep my eyes focused long enough on the greeting. Overall, it was a good greeting and I was graciously accepted.

3. Keep your journal updated, and keep working on your hand-shake, eye contact, and smile until you notice significant improvement. (Note: This is an excellent exercise to practice with someone. For example, I have practiced it with my wife and found it very helpful.)

CHAPTER 31

BEING LOVING

*"The more I traveled the more I realized that fear
makes strangers of people who should be friends."*
—Shirley MacLaine

L ove is by far one of the most important gifts of all. Love is a
quintessential quality that makes for a better world and makes
life worthwhile. *Love* can be defined as "a feeling of affection," "a
strong fondness or enthusiasm for something," and "being close
to someone or something." When it comes down to it, love is the
most sought-after quality in the world. It is a principal feature of
life in The Giving Zone and an ultimate positive process.

Wallace D. Wattles says this best in Science of Getting Rich:

> *A man's highest happiness is found in the bestowal of benefits
> on those he loves; love finds its most natural and spontaneous expres-
> sion in giving.*

Love is the opposite of hate. When we hate something we are
actually distant from it. Knowledge and love work closely together,
while ignorance and hate go hand in hand. That which we know
about and understand we will more easily love and feel close to.
That which we don't know about and misunderstand, we will tend

to feel distant from and may even hate.

This is a major factor in understanding many of the biggest problems on the planet. When people are ignorant, i.e., when people lack knowledge or understanding about something, they will automatically be distant from it and subject to hating it. This results in conflicts, divisions, and wars. Practicing ignorance and hate rather than love and understanding also causes divorces and business failures.

Loving involves getting close to someone or something. This is accomplished through understanding. What you know, understand, and get close to, you can embrace and you can have. What you have ignorance about, do not understand, and do not get close to, you tend to reject and can't have.

It is very enlightening to see how this applies to the various issues in our lives. Money is one such subject.

If people are ignorant about money they will not understand money. They will feel distant from it and unconsciously reject it. This helps explains why so many people are broke. Remember the example of the man who was raised in a family that believed that money was the root of all evil. They struggled financially because unconsciously they didn't want to have money and thus be evil. His ignorance and lack of understanding about money made him feel distant from it. His distance from money was synonymous to his unconsciously rejecting it. Thus, he couldn't have or keep much money so he suffered perpetually from being broke.

The subject of ignorance brings us to the idea of prejudgment or prejudice. Many of us prejudge people before we know them. This is a major destroyer of love. We may decide certain people are no good, or we may feel that there is something different or negative about them. This prejudgment is also a chief destroyer of opportunities. Great opportunities may not come along very often. When we prejudge someone or something, we could be writing off an ideal opportunity for a life-changing friendship, a perfect career, or any number of other open doors.

Making prejudgments is a form of hatred. When we make up our minds about people even before connecting with them, we feel very distant from them.

When we think we are right, our prejudgments intensify. Prejudice blocks the flow of love. Many people prejudge not only various people they meet, but also spouses, family members, friends, and co-workers. An awareness of our prejudices is essential to our ability to cultivate love.

This does not mean that we need shouldn't be discerning. There are some situations in which we need to use our judgment to protect ourselves from negative circumstances. However, let us be careful, and let us be slow to judge, before we make a mistake we may regret.

> *I have been guilty of this many times. And when I catch myself in a prejudgment, I really feel foolish. There have been a number of times that I have prejudged people when I first met them. I prejudged one person in a business I'm involved with. When I first met him, I thought that he didn't have much going for him. He seemed kind of quiet and ordinary. However, in a relatively short time, he became CEO of that organization. Quiet and ordinary were assumptions I had made immediately without even talking to him. These assumptions were prejudgments and not based on truth.*

I have come to realize that my prejudgments are many times far from accurate. Learning to catch my judgments and open my eyes to their inaccuracy has been a key focus of mine for many years.

> *Once I was at a meeting listening to a speaker. There was a person near me who was dressed plainly, so I figured she was probably something like an office clerk. I decided to talk with her to get beyond my prejudgment. It turned*

out that she was a successful executive in a corporation. It surprised me how far off I was.

A very powerful way to begin to let go of prejudice and the workings of an overly critical mind is to understand that what we prejudge about another is usually triggered by something we dislike about ourselves.

If we don't like something in ourselves, we tend to dislike that same or similar quality when we see it in another person. An effective way to become aware of these issues is to make it a practice to first look at our prejudgments as they occur. Immediately after catching the prejudgment, we need to spot the characteristic in ourselves that is similar or related to the quality we have assumed describes the other person.

Here is an exercise that allows you to become aware of and thus move beyond your prejudgments. For years, I have used this exercise many times to overcome prejudices and a tendency to be overly critical. You can do the exercise yourself, or someone else can communicate it to you. The exercise works for people we don't know as well as for people we do know. It is actually very beneficial to do this exercise on the people you already know.

1. What do I prejudge or dislike in another person?
2. Tell me about that.
3. Have you ever done that very thing, or something similar?
4. If so, what have been the consequences (results)? List the consequences until you've had a realization of something important that gives you a deeper understanding.

Dustin decides a man he just meets is lazy because his clothes are a bit untidy. After doing the above exercise, he realizes that he himself has been lazy before in his life, particularly one time recently when he was unemployed and didn't look for a job for several months. By doing the exercise, Dustin was able to let go of his prejudgment about the man he had just met and give him another chance.

Again, life is very much like a mirror. What we perceive outside of ourselves so often is a reflection of what is inside. Thus, when we like or admire something about someone else, that similar quality is also likely to be within us.

The following opposite exercise can be useful for helping us bring out positive qualities within ourselves.

1. What do you like or admire in another?
2. Tell me about it.
3. Do you have that quality, or something like it within you?
4. If you would like to develop that quality further, think of at least two different ways you could accomplish that.

Elizabeth admires an artist she meets and especially likes her watercolor work. In doing the above exercise she recalls that she herself has an artistic talent. Years ago she expressed some remarkable talent in a pottery class she took.

The above exercises can help us increase our love and understanding. Write them down on a 3 x 5 card and carry it with you to remind yourself to ask these questions when you catch yourself making assumptions about someone, as well as when you see something you view as positive in another person.

Love is an ultimate gift to offer others and to encourage others to develop. Increasing our knowledge about subjects and people will greatly increase our love, because what we know and understand, we can get close to. Increasing our knowledge will also greatly increase our level of truthfulness. When we really know something, we understand it. When we understand it, we hold a much greater truth about it. Love, knowledge, and truth all work together to become one. This is an unbeatable power – a power we can possess when we participate in The Giving Zone.

CHAPTER 3 / EXERCISES

Reread this chapter and do the exercises recommended.

CHAPTER 32

GIVING TO CHARITABLE ORGANIZATIONS

"An ounce of action is worth a ton of theory."
—Ralph Waldo Emerson

To give something back to others is one of the secrets to having a prosperous, successful, and happy life, and to living in The Giving Zone. Many people get caught in the trap of everyday worries and do not think of giving to anyone else except themselves. This is a mental trap as well as a spiritual trap – because thinking only about ourselves actually is counterproductive to being effective in our lives.

It is actually the ability to focus outside of ourselves that is largely responsible for our success. Focusing only on ourselves disconnects us from others and will cause poverty – not only financially, but also in our relationships.

One of the biggest worries people have is in the area of finances. But if we just think about ourselves, we actually will not be able to get ahead financially.

Income is positively a result of service generated from focusing on others.

Our prosperity is a result of what we give. Many people think that prosperity comes from what you can get in life. *Just the opposite is true.*

Money is a form of exchange given to us for our services performed. For instance, when you earn your income at work, you are focusing on others' needs throughout the day. Truly successful salespeople put their attention on helping others to solve problems and helping them get what they want. Those successful in the restaurant industry focus on serving and pleasing customers concerning food. Successful teachers focus their attention on helping their students acquire knowledge. When such people serve others well, they are rewarded monetarily.

The truth is, the more you give, the more you receive. The more you give, the more your own needs will be met. Thus, as we give increasingly more time and more money, we will tend to increase our prosperity. This is the Law of Abundance: As you increase the amount you give to others, the more you can truly be wealthy – in friends, self-esteem, purpose, peace of mind, happiness, and finances.

In Chapter 2, I wrote about some negative programming I had been given by some boys in school who taught me that it was "uncool" to give. Fortunately, I have since been freed from this destructive pattern. My mother, a fairly well-known psychologist, taught me the concept of *social interest*. This is a term coined by Dr. Alfred Adler. Social interest means that we need to be interested in the welfare of our fellow men and women – family, friends, societies, nations, and the world. My mother taught me to think about how I could benefit others. I am very grateful to her for this. If each of us follows this Golden Rule, everyone is cared for.

One of my most cherished memories is when I was five years old my family and I were listening to a folk singer who sang the phrase, "One Brotherhood." At that moment I felt connected with all people everywhere. There are many times since then that I have continued to feel this "One Brotherhood" connection, and it compels me to continue in my strong desire to give and be helpful to others.

The people who give away lots of money, or lots of time, are the world's truly wealthy people.

They give abundantly and they receive abundantly. It is a universal law that what you put out is what you get back. As we've discussed before, the biblical lesson expresses an ultimate truth: *What we sow is what we reap.*

There are many charitable organizations that depend on financial contributions and volunteer help to assist others less fortunate. There are numerous religious organizations that depend on financial contributions and volunteer help for their existence. I believe that it is important for us to contribute to the organizations we believe in as much as we can.

Many years ago, I met a business leader who told me about the problems of charitable organizations that lack funding. The government helps the poor to a certain extent, but there are many needs which the government does not meet. Therefore, billions of dollars are donated by wealthy individuals and businesses to the poor who need help to survive.

A great deal of money is also donated by many people in the middle class, and even by other poor people, who want to give what they can.

Because we reap what we sow, it is important to note that there are many benefits we can receive from giving money or time to charitable organizations.

There have been a number of times that I've given money to a charity and almost immediately my finances have surprisingly increased. This is not to say that one should give with the motive of getting back. It is much better to give wholeheartedly from the joy of giving without expecting something in return.

I donated some money to an organization that helped people who were affected by Hurricane Katrina. Within a day, I suddenly had personal income coming in unexpectedly. Some may say it's a coincidence. But I believe it makes perfect sense. There is a spiritual reality as well as a physical reality that operates in the world. The spiritual reality does not follow the perceptual and logical laws of physical reality. The spiritual reality is well worth looking at, since it contains more truth than the physical reality. It pertains to the essence and uniqueness of who we are, and the essence of what we are here to accomplish, as well as the essence of a Higher Power. The benefits of understanding the spiritual reality can be great in increasing the quality of our lives and the quality of our giving to others.

Another benefit to giving our time or money to a worthy cause is the people we can meet who are connected to a particular organization. When my wife and I have attended fundraisers, we have often met outstanding individuals.

Also it can be lots of fun to be involved in charitable organizations. It's fun to go to the social events connected to charities. There are great speakers, auctions, and prizes. The atmosphere makes it especially fun to give. Another benefit to helping a charitable organization is that we can learn new things. Knowledge gained from participating in a charity can be very enjoyable and interesting, taking us on all sorts of adventures.

I helped one charity a couple of times by volunteering to sell raffle tickets. My job was to walk up to people at a particular fundraising event to inspire them to buy tickets to raise some funds. However, I did not know how to be effective in selling the tickets so I felt a bit nervous. This did not help me sell tickets.

I asked the head of the charity to show me how he sold the raffle tickets. He had me watch him. I watched how masterful he was when he walked up to people; he was very straightforward and relaxed, and he used humor. It took me a while to catch on, but as soon as I started to relax and joke around, I could connect with people better. This lesson has also proved helpful to me in other areas of my life.

It feels great to know that you've made a contribution to others' lives. It automatically causes an increase in self-esteem and self-worth. When we feel good about ourselves, our prosperity increases.

When we have feelings of low self-worth and low self-esteem, we tend to be less prosperous. When we have feelings of high self-esteem and high self-worth, we tend to be more prosperous.

Giving to causes we believe in can also be an effective way of making restitution for past mistakes. For instance, people who have survived drug and alcohol problems may want to do volunteer work to help others suffering with the same addictions.

Community organizations in towns across the country are a valuable way to contribute to a worthy cause. These organizations are great places to form friendships, to network, and to learn. They usually have weekly speakers and they have community charitable events to raise funds for schools, hospitals, etc. Such organizations include Rotary International, Kiwanis International, The Exchange Club, The Optimists Club, Lions International, and Business and Professional Women's Club, Inc. Visit *www.guidestar.com* for all sorts of descriptions of charities across the country. Let's each find new ways to give our time and resources to making a better world and bringing more and more participants into The Giving Zone.

CHAPTER 32 EXERCISE

The purpose of this exercise is to have each of us examine the ways we would like to give more of our time and/or money to charitable organizations. Included in charitable activities can be helping a neighbor, relative, or friend who has a need.

1. Make a list of the benefits you would provide as well as receive by becoming more involved in charitable work. Keep writing down these benefits until you've had a noticeable shift in your awareness.

2. Make a list of the abilities, skills, and talents you possess that you would like to contribute toward charities you believe in.

3. Pick one or more charities that you would like to become involved in or more involved in. Decide what you would like to do for the charities and form a plan. You may need to do some research on the types of charities that you would like to be involved with, and then find out what types of volunteers they're seeking and what fundraising needs they have.

4. After you've done your research and formed a plan, you can now implement your plan.

CHAPTER 33

GIVING TOGETHER IN MARRIAGE AND FRIENDSHIPS

"Communication that contains the correct estimation of truth will capture anyone's attention and hold them spellbound."
—Alan C. Walter

*I*n September 2005, my wife and I received special recognition for the contribution to a particular organization we belong to and had been helping over the past 16 years. She and I worked together to help the organization in many ways.

When married couples have projects they work on together, they are more likely to have a very strong relationship. The same is true for friendships. Two or more friends who join together to help with some cause or to contribute in some way will tend to have strong and lasting friendships. Also they can be co-directors of winning stage productions in their lives.

There is magic when two or more people come together to contribute toward some endeavor. Each couple or group who works together effectively adds more territory to The Giving Zone. The bigger we can make The Giving Zone, the better the world will be for all of us to enjoy.

It is interesting that the foundation of our marriage was founded on giving and contributing. My wife and I met in an educational setting in which we taught relationship classes together. Through teaching these classes, we formed a strong friendship and fell in love.

Our wedding vows included our goal to serve humanity. This core purpose has created a very powerful bond that has always given us a significant reason to be together. Like any marriage of 18 years, we've had our ups and downs; however, our union is founded on the virtue of giving. This higher purpose keeps us together and helps create a very deep bond of love.

Many marriages are based exclusively upon romance and sex. These can be good qualities to share. Yet, there are other stronger qualities that will make a marriage so resilient, it is much more likely to last. For instance, when a couple comes together to raise a family, run a business together, contribute to others in some way, etc., a higher purpose can come into play and help to make a lasting relationship.

One quality that will tend to improve when married couples contribute to an activity together is communication.

The quality of communication in a marriage makes or breaks a marriage. Many couples do not communicate very well. After a year or two, they may find themselves having little to talk about. Worse, they may be so bored that the only way they may find relief from the agony of boredom is to pick fights. Unconsciously, they destroy their marriage through fighting in a desperate attempt to seek excitement.

On the other hand, when couples choose to have projects they participate in together, the quality of their communication can improve. Suddenly they see new meaning and purpose. High-quality communication is a direct result of purpose.

Purpose drives any activity. If a couple can unite with one purpose bigger than themselves, their communication will improve and their marriage will improve. Such a purpose can not only include charitable work, a business, or raising a family, but any other project completed together. When this work is also enhanced by the individuals' spiritual practice, their work can often be even more effective.

The married couples that my wife and I know who work together to contribute to something of great value tend to have a very strong bond. Purpose is like a glue that keeps people together.

If you're having troubles in your marriage, consider doing projects together.

Take a class together. Start a business. How about doing volunteer work together as part of an organization you both believe in?

This same principle also applies to friendships. Some friendships are superficial. These friendships often lack purpose. When friends decide to take up a cause together, it can help them form a strong and meaningful bond.

For example, friends who love sports can do volunteer work with children and sports. Friends who share a common religious/spiritual affiliation can participate in their activities. When a group of friends is business-oriented, they can get involved in a fundraising project. Those who love doing things with their hands may decide to become involved in Habitat for Humanity, which builds homes for families who are struggling economically. And friends who love animals can get involved in organizations that help protect animals.

Find a common interest that includes an aspect of giving of yourselves, and your relationships will deepen with renewed purpose. You'll be able to make lasting and joyful connections living in The Giving Zone.

CHAPTER 33 EXERCISE

This exercise is designed to encourage you to work together more on projects with important people in your life. These projects could be mutually beneficial not only to you, but also to the people your project is designed to help.

1. Is there someone in your life with whom you would like to work together on a special project?

2. Select a project you would like to work on. This could range anywhere from working together to help a charity to working together in a business to taking a class together, etc.

3. Make a list of the benefits you could get from working together on this project. Write down these benefits until you've had a realization of something important that has given you a deeper insight.

4. Write down a plan including the steps you would like to take to get the project going.

5. Implement the plan.

CHAPTER 34

GIVING AND RECEIVING IN HARMONY

"Real riches are the riches possessed inside."
—B.C. Forbes

Those who truly are great in their ability to give are also accomplished in their ability to receive. When we can achieve a balance in both giving and receiving, we create a rare type of harmony in our lives. This harmony and balance, a very positive process, causes a constant flowing back and forth of very creative and dynamic positive energy.

This is a key part of the dynamics of living in The Giving Zone. Participants enjoy a journey of abundant giving and receiving. It builds, and it is perpetual.

This exciting dynamic requires a balance of both giving and receiving so that the flow of energy can continue. Otherwise, nothing happens. The qualities of both giving and receiving are like the terminals of a battery. Giving is the positive pole and receiving is the negative pole. To give and not receive, or to receive and not give, short-circuits the flow of energy.

As we discussed earlier, upsets in life occur when there isn't equitable exchange involved. For example, if we give and get nothing back in a relationship, we will likely feel upset. If we take and give nothing back in a relationship we will also likely feel upset because we will feel a sense of obligation to give something back.

Alan C. Walter says:

An upset acts to short circuit the power flow...

This short circuit will result when there is inequitable exchange. Our power is slowed down or stopped when the other person receives something of value from us and won't give anything back, or gives something of value to us and won't receive anything back.

There are people who give freely and will not receive anything back. This will cause major problems in the flow of exchange and the flow of power. If everyone were just giving and no one were receiving, it would be difficult to accomplish anything. Here's an example:

Steve and Jane are production managers in an office. Their boss wants his employees to work as a team. Steve tries to give Jane a compliment about her proficient writing ability. Jane refuses to accept it, saying it's not necessary to give her praise. She does try, however, to give something to Steve. She offers to help him figure out how to use a new difficult piece of software that she is familiar with. He refuses to accept her help because he feels he should be able to figure it out himself. He wastes several hours struggling to figure out the software.

Steve later offers to help Jane solve some bookkeeping problems. Jane says, "No, thank you." She doesn't feel it's necessary for him to help. She also struggles for hours, wasting valuable time.

Steve is beginning to feel frustrated that Jane will not allow him to give to her. Jane, sensing this, offers to help Steve by proofing a business report he had written earlier in the day. Steve tells her that she needn't bother to help him.

Jane feels slighted that Steve refuses her help. Both Steve and Jane leave the office that day feeling unfulfilled and irritated. They also notice that their production quotas are far lower than expected.

The following example, on the other hand, illustrates what happens if Steve and Jane were to give and receive freely.

Steve gives Jane a compliment about her proficient writing ability. Jane thanks him for the compliment. Jane soon after notices that Steve is struggling with a difficult new piece of software. She offers to help him figure out how to use the software. Steve is happy to get her help and it saves him several hours' time.

Later Steve offers to help Jane solve some bookkeeping problems and Jane helps Steve proof a business report. Both Steve and Jane are energetic, productive, and upbeat.

Furthermore, their attitude of giving and the joy they feel affects the other employees in the office. The other employees are inspired and start working more as a team by helping each other. The production of the office soars and the employees enjoy their work.

There is no shame in receiving as long as it's in balance with giving. One cannot exist without the other, because it's a continuous ebb and flow.

The subject of romance gives us another example of the ebb and flow of giving and receiving. A woman who is attracted to a man at a party gives him a smile. He is happy to receive her smile and gives a smile back. She receives his smile and gives him a compliment about his tie. He thanks her for the compliment and tells her that she has a beautiful smile. The two people continue giving and receiving positive communications and suddenly it's as if there is no one else at the party. They exchange phone numbers and plan to get together for dinner the next evening.

The give and take, ebb and flow, applies to all of life's relationships – from coaching team sports to teaching to parenting to running a business. The list is endless.

Napoleon Hill writes about the concept of the "Master Mind" in which like minds get together in a harmonious fashion with a common purpose to combine their creative ideas and resources in order to implement projects greater than themselves.

He says in *Law of Success*:

A "Master Mind" may be developed by a friendly alliance, in a spirit of harmony of purpose, between two or more minds.... Out of every alliance of minds,...there is developed another mind which affects all participating in the alliance. No two or more minds ever met without creating, out of the contact, another mind...

Hill continues to explain that where great success is achieved, the Master Mind principle is involved. A number of people work together as one mind to create something of great value. Part of the magic of the Master Mind is that the individuals involved can give and receive freely and harmoniously. This does not mean that there aren't moments of conflict to work through. Conflict is part of the process. The people involved bring up differing points of view and will work through some disagreement to achieve a harmonious result.

Scientifically this is also true. An example of how conflict is necessary to make things happen is the sail of a sailboat. If there is no wind forcing itself against the sail, the boat will only drift.

The key is to be able to work through the differing points of view, which naturally will come up. This is an invaluable skill to develop that pays great dividends. The greater your skill in maintaining a positive ebb and flow at giving, the quicker the differing minds will meld together in the spirit of the group to become one mind, and the quicker you will all be key players in The Giving Zone.

When we can give and take freely as part of a Master Mind, we can make valuable contributions to help make a better world.

CHAPTER 34 EXERCISE

The purpose of this exercise is to continually increase your ability to give and receive fully. For example, in the area of love, if you could continually increase your ability to give and receive love, you would have very rich relationships. If you could continually increase your ability to give and receive money in connection to a valuable service, you could become very wealthy.

1. Name an area in your life in which you would like to continually increase your ability to give and receive.

2. What would be the consequences (results) of your being able to continually be able to give and receive in this area? Write down these consequences until you have a realization of something important that gives you a deeper insight.

3. Form a plan with steps on how you can become able to give and receive more in this area in your life.

4. Implement the plan.

CHAPTER 35

USING HUMOR

"The human race has only one effective weapon,
and that is humor."
—Mark Twain

*H*umor will reward you and the people with whom you come in contact with an abundance of extraordinary gifts. Humor will always brighten up serious situations.

Research has shown that the power of humor is so great that it can help heal disease. The research of Norman Cousins is famous in this regard. Cousins had cancer. He watched many comedy films such as The Marx Brothers, and laughed his way to health.

Humor also chases away gloom and anger. Jay Leno says:

You cannot be mad at somebody who makes you laugh — it's as simple as that.

I went to my hair stylist and she was not happy because there were hardly any customers that day. She said to me that business always goes down when there is a change in the weather. I answered jokingly, "You could put a sign on your window that reads that you offer discounts for changes in the weather." This statement was so ridiculous, she laughed uproariously.

Then I said, "why don't you put an advertisement in the newspaper that you will offer a discount for hair styling when the weather changes?" She again laughed out loud and her mood shot way up.

To look for the humor in life makes life a fun adventure. My wife and I were on a jet that had just taken off. The pilot said, "We now have the fasten-your-seat-belt sign turned off. Be sure to keep your seat belt fastened." This contradiction made me laugh. And this alone lifted my spirits.

Humor is a gift that wins people over and brings them together.

As a speaker, my goal early on in a presentation is to win people over. I share a humorous story very early in my speech. The laughter immediately turns reluctant spectators into attentive spirits who unite as one group focused on my message. At that point I have their undivided attention and can deliver my speech effectively.

Once I win over the audience through humor, I also lighten up inside and my speech has a life of its own, carrying me all the way through its various stages to a successful conclusion.

There are many other things that get people to laugh. One of them is laughing at the misfortunes of others. Laughing at the misfortunes of others can range from harmless comedy slapstick to laughing at someone else's dysfunction such as what you might hear from a stand-up comedian.

When we're in a low mood, we may be more inclined to laugh at the misfortunes of others. When we're in a high mood, we'll be more likely to laugh at more positive circumstances. We all laugh at exaggeration, and also at the unexpected.

One other thing that can bring on laughter is simply making yourself laugh – for no particular reason. If you are around other people, the laughter becomes a contagion propelling everyone to laugh. My wife and I heard Goldie Hawn give a speech once in which she conducted an exercise asking everyone to laugh spontaneously. She started laughing, and other audience members followed, laughing out loud. This is a great exercise you can do in a large or small group. As people really make themselves laugh, the laughter becomes unstoppable. I guarantee you'll all feel better.

Loy and Robert Young, writers of *Die Laughing – Is There Any Other Way? Laugh Your Way Through Your Senior Years*, have developed laughing exercises for individuals to do by themselves so that they'll be able to laugh uproariously on the spot. This exercise helps you raise your mood level, have fun, and exercise your laughing ability.

They also mention a very interesting phenomenon that explains a key part of what causes people to laugh. This has to do with the two hemispheres of the brain. The left brain is analytical, sequential, and logical. The right brain is creative, intuitive, and feeling.

This dichotomy contributes to a powerful mechanism that gets people to laugh. For example, a humorous story starts out with logical information that the left brain relates to. The punch line comes when something very illogical is shared that the right brain picks up on. In other words, this shift from the left brain to the right brain causes a spasm that can get the body to shake, and the person will laugh.

Larry Gelbart, writer/director/producer of the celebrated *M*A*S*H* television series says:

One doesn't have a sense of humor. It has you.

Give the gift of humor. Develop it and utilize it to the hilt. Humor is priceless – and it is a valuable asset both in The Giving Zone and on the stage of life.

CHAPTER 35 EXERCISE

The purpose of this exercise is to increase your ability to use humor and enjoy it. Pick any of the suggestions below that you would like to implement.

1. Collect humorous stories and jokes. Practice telling them by yourself. Then practice telling them to others.

2. Read books written to help us develop more humor.

3. Read books that contain humorous stories.

4. Watch comedians at work and study how they do their craft.

5. Watch classic comedy films and TV shows.

6. Write your own humorous stories and/or jokes.

7. Watch children play. Notice how they can be playful, silly, and naturally funny.

8. Practice being humorous. Look for humorous situations and use them to the max.

9. Put yourself in as many situations as possible that will get you to laugh, and let your laughter come out fully. Laughter is contagious and restorative.

10. Write down a number of ways humor benefits you and others in your life. Keep writing down these benefits until you've had a significant shift in your awareness.

CHAPTER 36

GAINING FULFILLMENT THROUGH PERSONAL GROWTH

"Love dies only when growth stops"
—Pearl S. Buck

What is a core quality of nearly all very successful people? It is that they are dedicated to their personal growth and to the personal growth of others. They read numerous books, listen to tapes, and attend workshops. They love to read biographies of famous successful people in order to glean inspiration. They are involved in mentoring others.

Benjamin Franklin led a life of personal growth. One of the things he was famous for is that he formed a personal-growth group of 12 people. They met regularly to help each other in their self-improvement in subjects including contributing to society and growing wealth by practicing principles such as honesty and frugality. They also enjoyed each other socially, and they simply had fun. From this group, and from later ones formed by its members, a number of services emerged which have benefited our society enormously – the first volunteer fire department, the first public library, etc.

A life of personal growth is paramount to having a contributing, prosperous, successful, and happy life. Your ability to continually improve is a measure of your aliveness. No growth equals no life.

Growth is synonymous with life.

I have identified two types of personal growth. One type is that which you do on your own. This includes books, tapes, the Internet, and other personal study and practice. The second type of personal growth is that which you get through the help of others. This would include seminars, classes, training, consulting, and coaching. Both types are important. However, the type of personal growth that will produce more improvement is the second. This is because it involves people outside of yourself, mentors who will interact with you and challenge you to change and grow.

Most people tend to stay within their comfort level and resist positive change. Therefore when they read books or listen to tapes, they will tend to gather information but only understand it and apply it according to the boundaries of their comfort zone.

Years ago, prior to my journey into personal growth, I was a very rigid person. This is because I was operating from a very limited comfort zone. Over the years as I've participated in many different types of personal growth, I've expanded beyond my comfort zone many times. This growth predominantly resulted from the seminars, training sessions, consultations, and coaching sessions I've attended. It was the personal and group mentoring that got me to see the limitations of my comfort zone and then to move through many of them. It also got me to let go of many fixed beliefs that were causing me to neglect using some of my key skills, abilities, and talents. Thus, I was able to learn new skills, expand my abilities, and help others improve at a much faster pace.

An example of the changes I made was that I used to be very shy. I would hardly ever talk to people I didn't know, and I was very scared to speak in front of groups. Now, I talk to people wherever I go, I love to host social events, and I can hardly wait for the next occasion to speak in front of a group.

My personal-growth objectives have included business, sales, relationship, and communication skills; letting go of past hurts; character building; teaching, coaching, and leadership skills; physical health; financial literacy; and spiritual improvement.

I would estimate that the gains I've made from the second type of personal growth are at least 100 fold over the gains I've made with the first type. Also, I've truly enjoyed myself and had a lot of fun during the mentoring I've received. Many times I can hardly wait for the next seminar or coaching session.

Again, we tend not to be able to see beyond our nose when it comes to our own limitations. It usually takes caring, trained people who can help us move outside of those boundaries. I've been very fortunate to have found some of the best mentors on the planet to work with me. Just as in other areas of life, you can find people who are very inexperienced and lack skill in mentoring, or those who are very experienced and consummate in their mentoring skills. I am continually searching for great mentors. I like to say that I am continually building a mentor bank. I have mentors in business, sales, relationships, leadership, finances, writing, etc. You will begin to find the mentors who are right for you as soon as you make the decision to seek them out.

I believe that having great mentors is a form of wealth. Mentoring is paramount for experiencing success. The people I know who work with mentors as much as possible are some of the most interesting, fun, contributing, loving, and adventurous people I've ever met.

Ideally, part of the mentoring process is taking what you've learned and passing it on to others. This is because when you help others learn what you have learned, you really get that knowledge yourself at a much deeper level. You know it, and then you feel it at the depth of your soul, because you've demonstrated that knowledge by helping another person get that knowledge too. For me this is one of the greatest joys and pleasures in life. When I help others attain their dreams, goals, and aspirations, I experience a happiness and a fulfillment that is unlike any other. For me, it is the epitome of satisfaction.

And on top of that, I will often advance in my personal improvement as much or more than the people I help. There are many people who say that we actually learn more during the teaching process than we do while being the student. This is a big reason why I've made a career out of helping people attain their dreams, goals, and aspirations. There is a tremendous gift in getting back so much from helping others improve. It is pivotal to the power and magic of living in The Giving Zone.

I encourage you to do your research and find the best mentors available. Interview them, and interview some people they've helped, to get a truer sense of their viability. Also, see if other top-notch mentors recommend them. One thing I like to do is find the mentors of the mentors. These are the people to really look for. Skilled mentors may spend a lifetime honing their skills. They also often spend years seeking top mentors for their own personal growth.

If you are ready to take a giant step in the advancement of your life, and you are ready to move more fully into The Giving Zone, I also encourage you to become a mentor to help others improve their lives. If you are already currently helping people as a mentor, I encourage you to continually improve your mentoring skills and abilities.

I also encourage you to find books and tapes that can help you in your own personal growth. The reading of books and listening to tapes is a very important part of personal growth. It expands your knowledge and it's something that is easy to work into your schedule. A great place to listen to tapes is when you are driving. You can even take courses by listening to tapes as you drive.

The mentoring I've received and the books and tapes I've studied have been fundamental to the giving process for me. For example, it was through mentoring that I learned about tacit sabotage, being myself, embracing failure, letting go of blame, building character, finding my life purpose, etc. As I work to master these challenges, I have increasingly become a better person, and a stronger participant in The Giving Zone.

There is always much more to give, and there is always much more to learn. Life has been a great adventure, and I have a lot of gratitude for the journey. I'm grateful to work toward improving my ability to be a worthy contributor in The Giving Zone, and I invite you to join me. There's plenty of room for anyone ready to find out how worthwhile and rewarding it can be.

CHAPTER 36 EXERCISES

These exercises can help you build a very good mentor bank, and also help you become a highly skilled mentor yourself. You will become very enriched from this process.

EXERCISE ONE

1. Make a list of the areas in your life where you would like to become very skilled.

2. Decide which areas you would like to work on with a mentor.

3. Begin to build or add onto your mentor bank. Some suggestions are: 1) Ask people you respect to recommend mentors they especially value. Especially ask people who actively seek mentoring. 2) Find various mentors and ask them who their mentors are. 3) Read books and listen to tapes. When you find particular mentors from the books or tapes that you admire, contact them to see if they would be willing to mentor you or if they would recommend other mentors. 4) Keep an open mind. Once you decide to seek a mentor, one could appear in your life in the least expected circumstances.

4. When you locate possible mentors, ask them questions about their experience, training, and working style to check for their skill level and their compatibility.

5. Have fun!

EXERCISE TWO

1. Make a list of skills and abilities you possess that you would like to share with others as a mentor. Some examples may be leadership, finances, business, computers, character development, religious/spiritual practice, humor, teaching, personal

growth, happiness, etc.

2. If there are skills you haven't fully developed yet, but you would still like to help others improve in those skills, make a list of them. Go back to Exercise One (above) and form a plan to attain one or more of those skills so that you will later be able to mentor others.

3. Make a list of areas in which you would like to help others improve. Some examples may be leadership, finances, business, computers, character development, religious/spiritual practice, humor, teaching, personal growth, happiness, etc.

4. Select mentors to help you improve these skills as well as to teach these skills.

CHAPTER 37

FORMING A GIVING CIRCLE

*"I'm looking for a lot of men who have
an infinite capacity to not know what can't be done."*
—Henry Ford

What kind of a world would we have if we were all genuine participants in The Giving Zone? What if each of us created circles of giving with those around us?

In a Giving Circle, people get together in groups to give to others. It is a term particularly connected to charitable work. There are many forms of Giving Circles. Each person gives something of value to others, and the flow of the Giving Circle eventually returns the giving to those who give, and it builds and builds.

Today, the most common form of a Giving Circle consists of a group of people getting together for philanthropic purposes. For example, someone calls her friends and forms a Giving Circle for the purpose of donating money to a particular charity. Perhaps 10 people join. They may decide to each donate $500 or $1000 per year to this charity or they may set it up so that people donate based upon what they can afford.

I am fascinated that some Native American tribes had a type of Giving Circle naturally built into their culture. Some of the tribes in the prairie lands had a very powerful concept of wealth. Their view of wealth was defined by how much you give, not by how much you have. Thus they were living in a Giving Circle, one person giving to another and another, ad infinitum.

Geese form a Giving Circle when they fly long distances. Warren Wilson describes it in *5-Step Problem Solving*.

Let's honor others as the geese do:

- As each bird flaps its wings, it creates uplift for the bird immediately following. By flying in a V formation, The whole flock adds 71% greater flying range than if each bird flew on its own.
- People who share common direction and sense of community can better get where they are going more quickly and easily because they are traveling on the thrust of one another.
- When a goose falls out of formation, it suddenly feels the drag and resistance of trying to go it alone.... and quickly gets back into formation to take advantage of the... lifting power...
- When the lead goose gets tired, it rotates back into formation, and another goose flies point. It is sensible to take turns doing demanding jobs.
- Geese honk from behind to encourage those up front to keep up their speed....
- Finally, and this is important.... when a goose gets sick, or is wounded by gunshots and falls out of formation, two other geese fall out with that goose and follow it down to lend help and protection.
- They stay with that fallen goose until it is able to fly again, or it dies.

Wilson explains that like geese we are interdependent on each other and that we need to stay in formation with those that are going in the same direction as we are. He also says that we need to stand by each other in tough times and be willing to give help and receive help like geese do.

I included the above passage because it is remarkable. It is something to be read many times. There is much to learn from it and there are many ideas we can draw from it and apply in our lives.

Skye Thomas provides a good description of the Giving Circle and how it works. This description comes from his newsletter called *Tomorrow's Edge*:

> The rules of the Giving Circle are simple. You must have a void of some type that needs filled. You must be considered worthy and appreciative of the gifts being given. You have to keep the circle going by giving something else of equal or greater value. You may be a grandparent giving hugs and kisses that spread amongst the entire family and come back to you later from your children. You may be a businessman buying and selling goods and services. You get back what you have put into the Giving Circle. You usually do not get it back from the same person that you gave to. The circle loops around on itself.

Here is how I envision a perpetually expanding Giving Circle:

> *A group of 15 friends come together to form a Giving Circle. They each begin to donate money every month for a favorite charity. The average donation is about $75 per month. However, they want to involve multitudes of others in their Giving Circle. They write a newsletter. Each member commits to sending a newsletter to 30 friends who live within the area.*
>
> *The newsletter is about their Giving Circle, and it describes the many benefits to being part of their Giving Circle – the opportunity to be of service, to see results in changing people's lives, to be part of a dynamic group, to have fun, etc.*
>
> *The newsletter asks each person who receives it to make a minimum donation of $25 to the charity the Giving Circle has chosen. In return, they will each be honored at a special dinner that could include entertainment and dancing.*
>
> *At the special dinner, people have fun, they meet new people, and the next wave of the Giving Circle is launched.*

Each new participant is asked to send out 30 copies of the newsletter to 30 friends to help create the next even bigger event. In addition, several people who have connections in other parts of the nation step forth to start Giving Circles in those areas.

Other fun ingredients can be added to keep the Giving Circle ever-expanding, such as silent auctions, door prizes, speakers, group travel events, and discounts on special services for members.

In truth, and ideally, we are already involved in some level of Giving Circles – families, friends, groups, businesses, churches, synagogues, communities, etc. We can all become aware of what we are currently doing in the area of contribution that involves the Giving Circles of our lives.

I would like to invite each of you to join my Giving Circle related to this book. Read this book, pass it on, and share the parts that are meaningful to you with others. Pass along your gifts of being yourself, smiles, embracinig failure, being straightforward, gratitude, forgiveness, abundant giving, etc. and take up permanent residence in The Giving Zone.

I encourage each of you to help build up Giving Circles in your life, and to enjoy creating new ones.

Giving Circles can take many forms. Each one instantly puts people in The Giving Zone. What kind of world would we have if it really got going? What kind of stage productions in our lives would we be directing? What if each of us were to enact Giving Circles in our families, in our workplace, in our communities, and around the world?

Let us each go forth with our hearts firmly planted in The Giving Zone – and we'll expand its territory forever, making a better world for all of us.

CHAPTER 37 EXERCISE

In this exercise you can let your creativity loose and design the type of Giving Circle you desire. You are encouraged to let your thoughts go free.

1. Design the Giving Circle of your dreams. Have fun!

2. Design other Giving Circles if you like.

3. Be bold! Start your dream Giving Circle.

AFTERWORD

Now that you have finished this book, what are you going to do?

Your passion in the area of giving is strong and you want to strengthen it further. You have a burning desire to do more to participate in The Giving Zone, which can help you improve all areas of your life and help improve the lives of many people. What can you do to keep this passion burning inside you and keep the flame of The Giving Zone alive?

I have an idea:

Since writing *The Giving Zone*, I am grateful to be receiving deep appreciation for the different ways this book is helping people better their lives. This appreciation gives me the greatest satisfaction and a desire to give as much as possible in continuing our work together in The Giving Zone.

It is very possible that you have some burning questions, desires, and goals that are coming up for you in the process of reading *The Giving Zone*.

You may have questions such as:

- How do I further express these principles in my life?
- Where can I particularly focus on and enhance my giving talents?
- How can I start a Giving Circle and get others to participate?
- How can I teach The Giving Zone principles to others?
- How can I find out more about discovering my life purpose or dream?
- How can I use the principles of *The Giving Zone* to improve my success, wealth, relationships and happiness?

To address the questions, desires and goals that may be coming to mind, I am including a Website for you to visit to request a complimentary Giving Zone Analysis for those people who have read *The Giving Zone.*

You will be able to write out the specific questions, desires, and goals that you want to discuss, at the top of the first page of the analysis. They will be addressed. In addition, the Giving Zone Analysis will help you more deeply address your concerns by looking at your strengths, abilities, and areas in which you may want to improve. You will end up with a plan to help you address your specific concerns, and to take some steps toward attaining what you seek.

In addition, as part of the Analysis, if you supply your email address, you will receive a complimentary monthly Internet newsletter called *The Giving Zone.* This will provide you with ongoing support for your desires, goals, and plans, plus recommended reading and practical information related to living in *The Giving Zone.*

When you fill out The Giving Zone Analysis forms, please also indicate at the top of the first page if you are very dedicated to personal improvement and/or to giving at your highest potential. Also, if you are an owner or executive of a company, you are welcome to indicate the specific needs you have for your company.

To take your Giving Zone Analysis, go to *www.livinginthe-givingzone.com* and make your request for an Analysis by clicking on the button indicating that you have read *The Giving Zone*. Next, proceed to take the Analysis by first writing down your questions, desires, and goals, and then complete the questionnaire. Please answer the questions as honestly as possible.

If you are ready to go forward in maximizing your abilities, including your giving capacity, and we work together on The Giving Zone Analysis, you will be amazed and elated at how helpful it will be.

Whatever you do, it is my hope that you will dedicate yourself to fulfilling your life purpose, and to being an active resident of The Giving Zone.

If you would like to talk with me personally,
I can be reached toll-free at (866) 319-7736
e-mail me at *ba.painter@comcast.net.*
or write to me at
The Advanced Coaching and Leadership Center,
1400 Camp Letoli Road, Saint Jo, TX 76265

RECOMMENDED READING

These are books with positive principles, which I highly recommend.

The following books by Napoleon Hill are available at popular bookstores or you may order them online at *www.naphill.org*.

Think and Grow Rich, (Personal Growth, Wealth, and Success Strategies).
Law of Success (Giving Principles, Wealth, and Success Strategies).

The following books by Robert Kiyosaki are available at popular bookstores or you may order them online at: *www.livinginthegivingzone.com/richdad*.

Rich Dad Poor Dad (Wealth and Success Strategies).
Cash Flow Quadrant (Wealth and Success Strategies).
Rich Dad Smart Kid (Wealth and Success for Children).

The following three books by Alan C. Walter on personal growth are available only through Wisdom Publishing Company. They can be ordered through *www.livinginthegivingzone.com/books* where you can also read a description of each book:

The Secrets to Increasing Your Power, Wealth, and Happiness.
*Paradigm Matrix and its Effects on Future Prosperity and
    Human Events.*
*Effective Communication Skills – The Key to Upgrading Your
    Life and Relationships.*

The following book is available at popular bookstores:

How I Raised Myself From Failure to Success in Selling (Sales
    Training and Giving Principles), by Frank Bettger.

If you would like to order additional copies
of *The Giving Zone*, go to
www.livinginthegivingzone.com/orderbooks
or call toll-free 866-319-7736.

The Giving Zone is available at special quantity discounts
for those who wish to purchase in volume,
or to use as premiums and sales promotions,
or to use in corporate training programs.
For more information contact the author at
ba.painter@comcast.net
or at the above toll-free phone number.

ABOUT THE AUTHOR

Bruce Painter, owner of Bruce Painter Consulting Group, has been a speaker, consultant, and trainer for the past 33 years. His consulting has carried him to a range of locations including Australia, British Columbia, and Hawaii. Affiliated with the Advanced Coaching and Leadership Center, Bruce and his wife Shoshana Painter, who works with him, live in Frisco, Texas.

Bruce and his associates specialize in helping business owners, executives, salespeople, service groups, families, and other individuals increase their capacity to give, and to have more success, more time, more freedom, improved relationships, and more enlightenment – all adding up to a better lifestyle. Painter's core focus is helping people achieve their highest career potential as well as their personal dreams and aspirations.

His powerful message of living in The Giving Zone gives us all a roadmap for a contributing, winning, prosperous, and happy life.

For more information on customized on-site programs and speeches by Bruce Painter, or to inquire about his telephone conference-call training or phone coaching, call Bruce Painter toll-free at (866) 319-7736 or e-mail him at *ba.painter@comcast.net*.